The Tale of Genji

A READER'S GUIDE

Rutland, Vermont & Tokyo, Japan

WILLIAM J. PUETTE

❖ *The Tale*
of Genji

by Murasaki Shikibu

A READER'S GUIDE

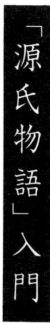

CHARLES E. TUTTLE COMPANY

Published by the Charles E. Tuttle Co, Inc.
an imprint of Periplus Editions (HK) Ltd.

LCC Card. No. 82-74088
ISBN 0-8048-1879-7

First printing, 1983
First paperback edition, 1992
Fifth printing, 1999

Printed in Singapore

DISTRIBUTION

North America
  Tuttle Publishing
  Distribution Center
  Airport Industrial Park
  364 Innovation Drive
  North Clarendon, VT 05759-9436
  Tel: (802) 773-8930
  Tel: (800) 526-2778

Japan
  Tuttle Publishing
  RK Building 2nd Floor
  2-13-10 Shimo-Meguro, Meguro-Ku
  Tokyo 153 0064
  Tel: (03) 5437-0171
  Fax: (03) 5437-0755

Asia Pacific
  Berkeley Books Pte. Ltd.
  5 Little Road #08-01
  Singapore 536983
  Tel: (65) 280-3320
  Fax: (65) 280-6290

Table of Contents

List of Japanese Chapter Titles with Translations

Where Waley and Seidensticker differ in their choice of chapter titles (whether English or Japanese), both are given in parentheses, with Waley's coming first. One title in parentheses indicates that their translations concur (with the exception of that for Chapter 38, ''Suzumushi,'' since this chapter was not translated by Waley). However, at the beginning of the chapter summaries in sections VI and VII, the Japanese chapter title will not be repeated as below. The reader should therefore consult this list to determine the title adopted by each translator.

1. Kiritsubo 桐壺 (Kiritsubo/The Paulownia Court) 62
2. Hahakigi 帚木 (The Broom Tree) 64
3. Utsusemi 空蟬 (Utsusemi/The Shell of the Locust) 67
4. Yūgao 夕顔 (Yūgao/Evening Faces) 69
5. Waka Murasaki 若紫 (Murasaki/Lavender) 73
6. Suetsumu Hana 末摘花 (The Saffron Flower/The Safflower) 76

List of Illustrations

Note: While premodern names are written in the traditional Japanese style (surname first), all modern names are written in the Western style (surname last).

Acknowledgments

I would like to express my deep appreciation to Richard K. Steiner for his invaluable help with the preparation of the manuscript and some of the illustrations, and for his and his wife Kimiko's most generous and gracious cooperation; to Professor V. Dixon Morris for his review of early drafts of the first two sections; to John Conner, who previewed sections of this work in his Japanese literature classes; to William Reed Richardson for his constant encouragement; to Elaine Kumano Young for her help retyping the manuscript; and most especially to my wife Carol for her drawing of the scene from the "Fujibakama" chapter, for her tireless work typing and retyping so many of the early drafts of this guide, and for her unflagging support and enthusiasm.

For permission to quote from the works listed, I wish to make acknowledgment to the following: Alfred A. Knopf, Inc. for the two excerpts from *The World*

13

of the Shining Prince: Court Life in Ancient Japan by
Ivan Morris, and the eight excerpts from Edward G.
Seidensticker's translation of *The Tale of Genji,* 1976;
Kodansha International, Ltd. for the two excerpts
from *Genji Days* by Edward G. Seidensticker; Houghton Mifflin Company for excerpts from *Diaries of Court
Ladies of Old Japan* by Annie S. Omori and Kochi Doi,
and for the U.S. rights to Arthur Waley's introductions
to, and translation of, *The Tale of Genji;* Walker and
Company for U.S. permission to reprint the two
excerpts from *Madly Singing in the Mountains* edited
by Ivan Morris; George Allen and Unwin, Ltd. for the
Canadian and United Kingdom rights to reprint the two
excerpts from *Madly Singing in the Mountains,* and for the
various excerpts from Arthur Waley's introductions
to, and translation of, *The Tale of Genji;* Dell Publishers
for *Japan from Prehistory to Modern Times* by John Whit-
ney Hall; University Press of Hawaii for *Japanese Poetry:
The "Uta"* by Arthur Waley; Columbia University
Press for *Sources of Japanese Tradition* by Ryusaku Tsuno-
da, William T. de Bary, and Donald Keene; Harvard
University Press for *Izumi Shikibu Diary* by Edwin
Cranston, copyright 1969; the Centre for East Asian
Cultural Studies for *The Vocabulary of Japanese Literary
Aesthetics* by Sen'ichi Hisamatsu; Stanford University
Press for *Introduction to Japanese Court Poetry* by Earl
Miner; Charles E. Tuttle Co. for *Art, Life and Nature in
Japan* by Masaharu Anesaki; Monumenta Nipponica for
Earl Miner's article "Some Thematic and Structural
Features of the Genji Monogatari."

Acknowledgments are also due to the following: Oxford University Press for permission to reproduce the illustration of court instruments from *A History of Japanese Music* by Eta Harich-Schneider (pp. 34–35); Meiji Shoin Publishers of Tokyo, Japan for their permission to reproduce illustrations from *Koten Zukan* by Isoji Aso (pp. 2–3,30); Tokyodo Publishers for permission to reproduce illustrations from *Genji Monogatari Jiten* by Kikan Ikeda (pp. 31, 115, 179); Professor Bun-ei Tsunoda of the Heian Museum of Ancient History for his invaluable direction and advice.

かゝる、世の
古事ならでは、
げに、何をか、
紛るゝことなき
つれづれを慰めまし。

Were it not for these old romances,
what would we do to beguile our idle hours?
—Genji Monogatari, *"Hotaru"*

Introduction

This book is intended to be a reader's guide to the Arthur Waley and Edward G. Seidensticker translations of *The Tale of Genji* by Murasaki Shikibu.

As the world's oldest novel and, in the words of Nobel laureate Yasunari Kawabata, as "the highest pinnacle of Japanese literature," this eleventh-century romance has long been read and admired by students of world literature as well as by Japanophiles. The recent retranslation by Seidensticker has excited even more interest, but students and would-be teachers still may hesitate at a study of the work, lacking confidence in their ability to analyze it, being ignorant of its historical and cultural milieu.

So deep is the gulf between the world of *The Tale of Genji* and the world we live in that even modern Japanese cannot read the work in the orginal form without special study. It is believed by some scholars that the very language spoken by Japanese of the Heian period had sounds no longer contained in modern speech. Today, the Japanese themselves must, therefore, read modern renderings of the work. But at least they are able to resort to a considerable body of scholarly research in the form of charts, concordances, and all manner of guides. How much more, then, should the Western reader require some guidance through the curious intrigues of the Heian court.

While Ivan Morris's text, *The World of the Shining Prince,* does go into intricate detail about the period, it does not particularly focus on the Tale and, at 329 pages, it is so formidable a study in itself that, added to the original task of reading the novel, at over a thousand pages, the book has not been fully utilized.

Clearly, what is needed, as Edwin Cranston of Harvard University pointed out in his review of the Seidensticker translation,[1] is a "Companion to Genji." The work I have prepared is designed to serve the average English-speaking reader of either translation. Furthermore, I concentrate on the first nine chapters, for they have been separately published in paperback and are more widely read. For these nine chapters I have written detailed summaries and thematic commentaries, which introduce some of the well-known themes, devices, and literary conventions of Murasaki's time, but leave considerable room for discussion and personal reflection.

I know from experience that students required to read only those first nine chapters are frequently curious to know how the Tale continues, so I provide summaries of the remaining chapters which I believe will satisfy a basic curiosity and, conceivably, stimulate a reading of the complete novel.

Most importantly, though, I present in this guide brief, illustrated essays on the historical, philosophical, and cultural features of the novel. Without at least a summary knowledge of such things as the Fujiwara bedchamber politics, the curious balance between Shintō and Buddhistic tenets, the pervasive concept of *karma* in human relationships and, most of all, the subtle aesthetics of *aware,* the major portion of this important novel would surely be lost on the average reader.

The notes I present on musical instruments, court dress, and the basic geography may not be as crucial to comprehension of the Tale, but will definitely add to its appreciation as well as expand the cultural awareness of the student interested in Japanese studies. Indeed, armed with these introductions, the Western reader may approach Murasaki's world without trepidation. The teacher of world literature may now be more inclined to lead a class through the work which, heretofore, he had himself found rather mystifying.

Finally, I have included a complete section on the

novel's characters, cross-indexed for both translations with transliterations of the Japanese sobriquets and epithets, so that the student who wishes to discuss or analyze the Tale, or even compare translations, will have a reliable list of the *dramatis personae* to avoid the confusion which naturally besets this complex plot.

My desire, therefore, is to provide an easily assimilable guide which lies within the means of the general reader. I have, it should be noted, taken the greatest pains to be as brief as possible, so that this classic of world literature, this shining jewel of Japanese literature, may be more readily available to Western readers.

PART ONE

The World of Genji

I

Heian Japan

Genji Monogatari is, many agree, the world's oldest novel, written a thousand years ago, but almost totally unknown to Western readers until the appearance of the fine translations of Arthur Waley and Edward G. Seidensticker in this century.

Before launching into a reading of this momentous work, it is important to have some grasp of the historical and cultural climate of the period of Japanese development that produced it. Ivan Morris makes the following crucial observation in his treatise, *The World of the Shining Prince*:

> If the informed Westerner was asked to enumerate the outstanding features of traditional Japan, his list might well consist of the following: in *culture* Nō and Kabuki drama, Haiku poems, Uki-yoe colour prints, samisen music, and various activities like the tea ceremony, flower arrange-

ment, and the preparation of miniature landscapes that are related to Zen influence; in *society*
the two-sworded samurai and the geisha; in
ideas the Zen approach to human experience
with its stress on an intuitive understanding of
the truth and sudden enlightenment, the samurai
ethic sometimes known as *Bushidō,* a great concern with the conflicting demands of duty and
human affection, and an extremely permissive
attitude to suicide, especially love suicides; in
domestic architecture, fitted straw matting *(tatami) ,*
large communal baths, *tokonoma* alcoves for hang-
ing *kakemono;* in *food,* raw fish and soy sauce. . . .
The list would of course be entirely correct. Yet
not a single one of these items existed in Murasaki's
world, and many of them would have seemed as
alien to her as they do to the modern Westerner.[1]

Indeed, the greatest barriers to the modern reader's
appreciation of this novel are the stereotypes and in-
valid preconceptions or expectations that we are likely
to impose upon it. Heian Japan (A.D. 794–1186)
was a period so unlike modern Japan, and so unlike
any other periods familiar to us, that we are obliged
to sweep away all of our preconceptions and try to
understand the world on its own terms, as we see it
in the novel.

The period is called Heian after the name of the
capital which in 794 had been moved from the old
site at Nara to eventually occupy the area which today
is known as Kyōto. The word "heian" 平安 means

"peace and tranquillity" and was adapted, as was the plan of the city itself, from the Chinese Tang capital at Chang-an 長安, occupying a six-thousand-acre mass of land approximately three and a half miles long and three miles wide.

The move, it is believed, was made because of the political grip that the Kegon sect Buddhist monasteries had obtained at Nara (then called Heijō 平城). Emperor Kammu, a Confucianist at heart, simply moved out from underneath them and established his court at Heian Kyō. There he enfranchised the less ambitious, more ascetic Tendai and Shingon sects, who were inclined to keep to their monasteries in the surrounding mountains outside of the city.

As the capital, this city was designed and built to accommodate almost exclusively the emperor and the ranked hierarchy of his court. Consequently, the world of *The Tale of Genji* is not really the world of Heian Japan at large; it is more accurately the refined world of the inner circle of the highest class in the land. In Chapter 2, for instance, when reference is made to the three classes, we should not make the mistake of supposing the reference was in large terms to the nation's aristocracy, its middle-class merchants, and its peasant farmers. Rather, as John Whitney Hall describes:

> The aristocracy as a whole. . . fell into three general divisions. The first three ranks were especially privileged and were available to only a few of the families closest to the imperial house.[2]

The great majority of people, not of the aristocratic class at all, were barely considered human, their appearance and language being so disparate. Conversely, at the top of the pyramid was the emperor and his immediate family whose majesty was so distinguished as to have them commonly known as "cloud dwellers" (*kumo-no-uebito*). In fact, whenever the emperor was depicted in drawings or picture scrolls, it was an artistic convention to show only the lower extensions of his robes descending from a heavenly mantle of clouds.

So centralized was this aristocracy at Heian Kyō that it became a kind of Mecca; indeed, for the privileged few, it was the only place of any worth. Throughout the Tale there abound references to the primacy of the capital. To a Heian patrician the worst possible fate was exile from its compound, and the worst possible stigmas on an aspiring aristocrat's pedigree would have been a vulgar origin in the provinces (i.e., anywhere but the capital) and countrified (*inakabitaru*) manners or speech. Unlike the previous Nara period, all that was worthy, noble, and beautiful was believed to reside exclusively in the capital. It was, then, truly a brilliant city and the focal point for all national development.

In the centuries just preceding this period, as a result of what is called the Taika Reform, the court had been involved in a wholesale absorption of practically all aspects of the illustrious Chinese Tang culture. At the Nara court all that was Chinese was so much in vogue that even the language was being conscientiously studied. Yet in the Heian period portrayed in *The Tale of Genji,* these Chinese systems and beliefs, having been digested, were in the process of essential modification to accommodate native Japanese sensibilities.

Confucianism was still the mainstay of formal education and so influenced the atmosphere at court that all formal edicts and even court poetry were composed in Chinese, as we see in Chapter 8, ''Hana no En.'' Unfortunately, this Confucian–Buddhist culture was primarily a male preserve. Women were deliberately excluded. Yet the political structure of Heian Japan was such that considerable influence and power were accorded to women of the aristocracy. So, while the men learned Chinese and studied the Confucian classics, Heian women were left to amuse themselves by mastering their native Japanese via the newly devised phonetic writing system and the Nara-period poetry anthologies. Of course, the men needed to know all these things as well so that they could deal socially with the women. As a result, the influence of Chinese began to wane, becoming more and more a specialized, exclusively masculine indulgence, less and less related to the realities of political connivance in court life.

On the other hand, women were important particularly because they were used to extend and infiltrate, by marriage, family- or clan-power cliques. The most famous and successful practitioner of this technique was the Fujiwara family, which had managed to be the prime supplier of imperial consorts during most of the Heian period. Before long, almost all of the emperors had Fujiwara mothers and Fujiwara wives, until the Fujiwara family was practically in control of the throne.

It is no surprise, then, to see the tremendous concern in the novel with marital alliances, for practically the only way of climbing the Heian social ladder was by securing a good match for one's offspring. Note how often fathers seem to throw their daughters at Genji's feet, hoping to match their fortunes with such an obviously promising prince, who was on the one hand clearly a member of the imperial family and, on the other, owing to his placement in the non-royal Gen clan, not beyond the reach of a reasonably well-bred aristocrat. To further simplify matters, polygamy was an accepted part of the social web. Though a single major marriage was usually arranged early in childhood, later, on the basis of personal preference, valid lesser marriages could be effected simply by mutual consent upon the third successful connubial visitation. However, for political reasons, a courtier with a wife whose family was powerfully connected at court, such as the Fujiwara, was less likely to enjoy a second or third marriage. Indeed, even an emperor's designs could be thwarted by the intrigues of the Fujiwara.

In *The Tale of Genji,* as a matter of fact, the Fujiwara clan is represented in the persons of Lady Aoi and Tō-no-Chūjō. It is interesting to chart the fortunes of their family in this powerful position as it moves through the three generations depicted; though we must be careful to remember that this is, after all, a novel focusing on manners and the high society of the

Heian court. The political events are generally peripheral to the plot.

DAILY LIFE AT COURT

For the denizens of the capital, the actual world of daily activities was, by comparison to ours, largely nocturnal, where time was solely governed by the flow of events. People slept, ate, and committed their other quotidian duties around their social activities, which more often than not were conducted at night, till just before dawn. Even the design of the buildings and furniture required that, for the most part, the courtiers lived out their lives in a state of semi-darkness, which certainly increases the significance of Genji's reputation as "the shining prince."

Indeed, so much was the woman's world shuttered and protected from the light of day, that simple identification could often be a difficult feat (note the "Oborozukiyo" episode in Chapter 8 as just one example). Women of the upper classes were scrupulously sheltered from public view by a plethora of screens and curtains, as well as by a retinue of ladies-in-waiting and attendants. Hence, eavesdropping and voyeurism, far from being considered perverted indulgences, were raised to a fine art.

There were, however, more artful means by which identification was possible. First, women of the court wore very elaborate and distinctive robes, layered and arranged tastefully so that color gradations and combinations could be admired in the long, dangling sleeves which were often allowed to project beneath their protective screens or from their carriage doors in transit, in a style referred to as *idashi-guruma*.

Second, as their robes were worn and slept in for extended periods of time, they were delicately incensed and perfumed with distinctive fragrances, especially created by the wearer, which could easily be recognized by anyone of good breeding. In fact, these garments could be so formidable that, as in the case of Nyōsan, the Third Princess of Suzaku, they might outweigh the inhabitant.

> Their lady was such a pretty little child of a thing, reduced to almost nothing at all by the brilliance of her surroundings. It was as if there were no flesh holding up the great mounds of her clothing.
>
> "WAKANA: JŌ," SEIDENSTICKER[3]

Screen (front and back views).

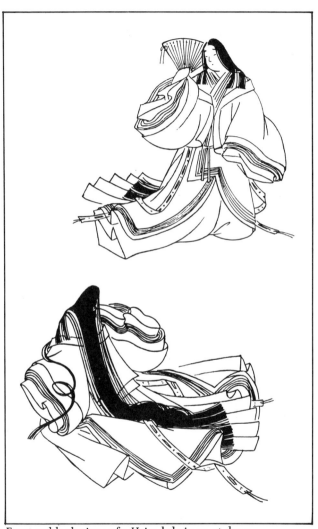

Front and back views of a Heian lady in court dress.

Little emphasis was placed on the physical features in judging the beauty of a lady. Her teeth would normally be blackened, and her generally plump face would be powdered white and artificial eyebrows painted over her real ones. Like classical European tastes, a slight corpulence was believed to enhance one's natural beauty. The only important physical trait that was admired and praised in poetry was a lady's hair, which was groomed to be at least as long as she was tall.

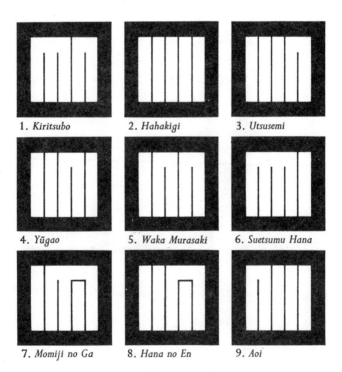

1. *Kiritsubo*   2. *Hahakigi*   3. *Utsusemi*

4. *Yūgao*   5. *Waka Murasaki*   6. *Suetsumu Hana*

7. *Momiji no Ga*   8. *Hana no En*   9. *Aoi*

Though not as obvious, there was one other way in which a courtier might be recognized in this twilight world. All members of the court were expected to acquit themselves as accomplished musicians on an array of instruments.

The most frequently described instruments in *The Tale of Genji* are the *koto* or zither, the lute, and the flute; and, of these, the *koto* is most often cited. There were, in fact, several varieties of this harp, and in the novel there are references to three basic types. The thirteen-string *sō-no-koto* was usually 190 cm. long or longer, made of oak or paulownia, and used movable bridges much like the modern day *koto,* though clearly it was borrowed from the Chinese *cheng,* as was the seven-string *(kin) koto* which Genji takes with him on his exile (Chapters 12 and 13). Although it was of Chinese origin, the thirteen-string *koto* is described as having a uniquely feminine sound. Interestingly, the popularity of the seven-string *koto,* of which Genji was an acclaimed master, paralleled his career, passing out of vogue with his demise.

Of special interest, though, is the third variety of *koto* mentioned in the novel, which was the native Japanese six-string *koto,* known variously as a *wagon, yamato koto,* or the Eastern zither *(azuma koto)* . This instrument could be anywhere from 105 to 210 cm.

(Facing page). Genji-kō crest designs for the first nine chapters. The ability to discern various incense fragrances was popular and highly developed in Heian Japan. Each fragrance (for the 54 chapters) had an individual incense burner with its own vent pattern. These patterns were later adopted as family crests.

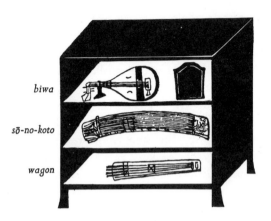

biwa

sō-no-koto

wagon

long and might be constructed of cypress or paulownia, with two resonance holes in the back. In the novel, Tō-no-Chūjō and his son, Kashiwagi, are credited as being particular masters of its use. The following passages from the "Wakana" chapters (34 and 35) indicate to some extent its character:

> It is rather the Japanese *koto*, the improvising after the dictates of one's fancy, all the while deferring to the requirements of other instruments, that fills the listener with wonder.
>
> "WAKANA: JŌ," SEIDENSTICKER[4]

> Though it is a rather simple instrument, everything about it is so fluid and indefinite, and there are no clear guides.
>
> "WAKANA: GE," SEIDENSTICKER[5]

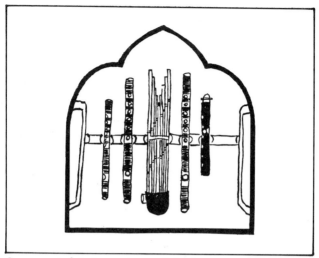

Court musical instruments stored in the proper manner (from an early scroll painting): string instruments *(facing page)*; wind instruments *(above)* showing the yokobue second from the left.

Indeed, compared to the rigid formality of the Chinese *koto,* the Japanese *koto* seems to have been a much more flexible, creative instrument.

The *biwa* is another Chinese import (the *p'i-p'a*), being a pear-shaped, five-stringed type of lute normally made of red sandalwood and usually measuring about 100 cm. in length. The *biwa* was often associated with wandering, mendicant priests, though it was definitely part of the standard court ensemble as well.

Finally, there was the bamboo flute or *fue,* of which there were many varieties, principally those played vertically and the transverse flute or *yokobue* (of Chapter 37) which is played horizontally. These varied in length and pitch, but averaged about 35 cm. long and usually had seven holes.

The musical quality of most of these instruments may, to the modern listener, seem piercing and harsh, but one can easily imagine how beautifully they were offset by the misty ambiguities of the Heian court; how much like the cicada these instruments enabled the quiet, unassuming souls of Heian lovers to penetrate the dead of night. For in this rather unique world of shadows and obfuscations (where, being secure for centuries in peace and stability, the culture had achieved its zenith) Murasaki herself lived out her life, and there created the world's first psychological novel of epic dimensions.

II

The Way of the Gods and the Three Foreign Teachings

In Heian Japan of the time that the *Genji Monogatari* was written, there existed a curious blending of several religious strains.

To begin with, the native religion of Japan is Shintō 神道, literally "the Way of the Gods," according to which all the beautiful and vital manifestations of nature are deified. Furthermore, the living souls of departed ancestors were believed to pass into nature, thereby linking man and nature in a mystic union. Life and the forces of life in nature were glorified. Likewise, death and its forces of decay were abhorred and regarded as pollutants. At the top of the Shintō hierarchy, then as now, is the emperor who, as living descendant of the Sun Goddess and, therefore, grand ancestor of all the Japanese, is the high priest of Shintō and purest representative of the Way of the Gods on earth. In fact, the overwhelming concern of Shintō is with purity. Most of its rites deal with purification and lustration. Taboos, known as *mono-imi,* result when people or things are defiled by such negative forces as death, disease, and even menstruation, requiring elaborate rituals to restore their purity.

Very early, though, from China and Korea came three major modifications to Shintō. The first of these was Confucianism (Jukyō 儒教) which had a vast political impact from about A.D. 645 with the issuance of various imperial edicts that came to be known as the Taika Reform. Though superficially Confucianism shaped the Japanese bureaucracy and even the map of the capital, its severe ethics had little permanent effect on Heian religious tenets. It is true that the Doctrine of Filial Piety, which dictates strict observance of the loyalty and honor that should exist between members of a family, did become especially popular as it tended to fit into the Shintō sense of ancestral sanctity, but the cool logic of the Doctrine of the Mean and the relentlessly dispassionate concept of "the virtuous bureaucrat" did not flourish in Japanese soil.

Taoism, pronounced *dah oh ism,* (Dōkyō 道教) on the other hand, did make a strong impression. The magical formulas of Taoist rituals, in particular, were so similar to the familiar Shintō ceremonies that the Japanese readily adopted the Taoist obsession with astrological and numerological codes, adopting as well the *in-yō,* or yin-yang, explanation of nature's dualism. The yin-yang, visually symbolized in the *tomoe* crest, expresses the notion that reality exists in the dynamic tension or balance struck between passive

The yin-yang (in-yō) symbol.

(yin) and active (yang) forces. Taoism further teaches that there is no true purity, that opposites tend to converge, for in the midst of yin there is always yang (note the little white circle in the black comma), as in the midst of yang there is always yin. Although this seems to run against the grain of Shintō belief, as ever the Japanese have happily accommodated paradox when the truth is keenly felt or intuited.

Perhaps the best example of this penchant for accepting the incongruous can be seen in the third and most influential import from China: Buddhism or Bukkyō 佛教. While it is true that Buddhism originated in India, the Buddhism that had found its way to Japan by the tenth century was clearly a Chinese product. When we talk about Heian Buddhism, we must be careful not to confuse it with the well-known Zen Buddhism, which did not develop in Japan until long after the Tale was written. The primary sects, as seen in the *Genji Monogatari,* were Tendai and Shingon (esoteric) Buddhism.

If some of the other religious ideas introduced to Japan had non-Shintō elements, Buddhism seemed its very antithesis. While Shintō had almost a phobia about death and decay, Buddhism seemed determined to encourage morbid reflection. The way of the Buddha is to seek salvation by enlightenment, that is, by realizing that the beauties of nature and the physical pleasures of life are illusory and transient (a concept known as *mujōkan*). Man's material and emotional desires only tie him to a continuous cycle of rebirths. To seek enlightenment, man must put aside the things of this world and concentrate on the holy word of the scriptures, primarily the Lotus Sutra.[1] All efforts made to achieve enlightenment can, even if enlightenment itself is not achieved, benefit one in the next incarnation, and, conversely, evil deeds will assuredly follow one as a curse from one existence to the next. This concept of moral causality is known in Sanskrit as *karma* (a term used often in the Waley translation, but scrupulously avoided by Seidensticker). To the Heian mind *karma* neatly accounted for the apparent inequities in the world: why one man, despite his virtue, seemed to have nothing but troubles to live with, or why another was blessed with continuous satisfaction. It was also employed to explain such strong emotional affinities as when one falls in love at first sight, for people once bonded together in a previous life were likely to be pushed together by the force of *karma*. In fact, the term is often translated as "fate" because the Japa-

nese were very fatalistic about the inevitable work-
ings of *karma*.

Thus, in Buddhism all people are encouraged to
put aside their family attachments (violating precepts
of filial piety), divorce themselves totally from their
material possessions, and take holy orders, so that
upon their deaths they may be reborn as Buddhas on
a lotus petal and escape forever the ignorance and desire of earthly existence. In *The Tale of Genji*, therefore, when reference is made to nuns and priests,
we must remember that these were not a special caste
or vocation as they are in Christian churches, but
ordinary members of the court who, feeling that their
lives or careers had come to an end, were preparing
themselves for the final step by renouncing the world
and trying to sever their karmic bonds.

III

"Aware" and Heian Poetics

Perhaps the most alien aspect of *The Tale of Genji* is the tremendous preoccupation of its characters with artistic pursuits. It is, in fact, impossible to exaggerate the importance of aesthetics in general, and poetry in particular, to the plot, theme, and character development of the novel. We might be familiar with other cultures in which virtues such as spiritual integrity, a ready wit, or simply military prowess figured so highly as to advance the esteem we would have of characters so endowed. But in *The Tale of Genji* the most important of all virtues, the aristocratic touchstone by which men and women at court were ultimately measured, was essentially their sensitivity to the inherent pathos of things, especially in the traditional arts.

This aesthetic was known as *aware* and is as difficult a term to translate as can be found. It has been variously defined:

. . . a word frequently used in *The Tale of Genji* and other classical literature. Among its wide range of meanings are "pathetic," "moving," "beautiful." The phrase *mono no aware* corresponds to *lacrimae rerum,* "the pity of things," which is often taken to be the underlying theme of Murasaki's novel.   MORRIS[1]

. . . exclamation of sympathy or distress.
                                                                    WALEY[2]

. . . an ejaculation of vague and undefined sadness.   SEIDENSTICKER[3]

In old texts we find it first used as an exclamation of surprise or delight, man's natural reaction to what an early Western critic of Japanese literature called the "ahness" of things . . . elsewhere it expressed a gentle sorrow, adding not so much a meaning as a color or a perfume to a sentence.   TSUNODA, KEENE, DE BARY[4]

The term suggests an anguish that takes on beauty or a sensitivity to the finest—the saddest—beauties. Both the condition and the appreciative sensibility are implied.   MINER[5]

. . . that which stirs cultivated sympathies by touching them with beauty, sadness, and the awareness of ephemeral experience.
                                                                    MINER[6]

. . . "an emotional awareness." *Aware* has a long history, from its origins in an exclamation expressive of admiration, surprise, or delight, to its modern meaning of "misery." In the Heian Period its most characteristic use was to express a feeling of gentle, sorrow-tinged appreciation of transitory beauty.   CRANSTON[7]

Originally an interjection ("Ah!" "Oh!"). From the Heian period on, it was used to express controlled feeling. As an aesthetic concept, it stands for elegance, or, at times, for pathos.
                                                HISAMATSU[8]

. . . an emotion of tender affection in which there is both passion and sympathy . . . in such moments the sentiment is instinctively felt, for in them joy mingles with a kind of agreeable melancholy.   ANESAKI[9]

It is also possible to understand this sentiment as an outgrowth of the religious conflict between the nature-worshiping creed of Shintō and the Buddhistic abhorrence of natural phenomena; the conflict between a philosophy urging oneness with nature on the one hand, against a philosophy urging transcendence of nature on the other. Caught in this ideological vise, the Japanese of the Heian period blended to their needs a sentiment which commanded a pathetic appreciation for illusory beauty.

As an aesthetic, it touched all of the arts and all of nature, but we see its most perfect expression in poetry. There are nearly eight hundred poems woven into the Tale, representing not the formalistic Chinese poetry composed by the males at court competitions, but the native Japanese *tanka* or *waka* (not *haiku*) form, consisting of thirty-one syllables. As is surely the case in all literatures, the linguistic peculiarities of the language largely determine the possible verse forms. We cannot expect sonnets to spill out of every tongue, nor was Chinese poetry particularly successful in the completely different character of Japanese speech, which is neatly described here by Amy Lowell:

> Japanese is a syllabic language like our own, but, unlike our own, it is not accented. Also, every syllable ends with a vowel, the consequence being that there are only five rhymes in the whole language. Since the employment of so restricted a rhyme scheme would be unbearably monotonous, the Japanese hit upon the happy idea of counting syllables. Our metrical verse also counts syllables, but we combine them into different kinds of accented feet. Without accent, this was not possible, so the Japanese poet limits their number and uses them in a pattern of alternating lines. His prosody is based upon the numbers five and seven, a five-syllable line alternating with one of seven syllables with, in some forms, two seven-syllable lines together at the end of a

period, in the manner of our couplet. The favourite form, the "tanka," is in thirty-one syllables, and runs five, seven, five, seven, seven.[10]

This poetry was usually composed in momentary flashes of inspiration. Most frequently, it was used as a subtle means of communication between lovers and friends, and was, therefore, an important part of daily life. Relying heavily on suggested meaning rather than overt expression, the images in these poems were used to hint at very subjective emotions, as people were often associated with flowers, trees, or other aesthetically acceptable images.

Furthermore, *waka* was composed according to accepted conventions that are difficult to discern even in the best translation. There was an extensive body of poetry from the Nara period already anthologized and circulated, and often a poet would use a well-known epithet, called a "pillow-word" or *makura-kotoba,* to describe a common subject or emotion. Or the reference might be more specific and allude directly to a famous poem, subtly changing a word or two to relate it to the new circumstances. This device was known as "allusive-variation" (*furu-kotoba* or *honkadori*) and was much admired when skillfully handled. Its recognition in the more obscure cases of its use was a sure test of breeding and discrimination, and Seidensticker's frequent notes attest to its popularity.

Finally, a poem might employ an elaborate pun or

sophisticated double entendre, called a "pivot-word"
or *kake-kotoba*. Careful manipulation of such a device
could provide a way for courtiers to suggest a more
explicit word which, by itself, might be considered
indelicate. Note the poem quoted by Shikibu in the
rainy night conversation (Chapter 2) in which his
intellectual lover used the word *hiru* for "day" in a
poem which also suggested *hiru*, "garlic," with which
she had been inadvertently blighted. And later in
Chapter 13, "Akashi," as the newly exiled Genji is
at last able to see the remote island of Awaji, the island's name becomes a literary nexus, and the beauty
of the acclaimed coast now mixes with the sting of
his banishment in this *waka*:

> *Awa to miru*
> *Awaji no shima no*
> *aware sae*
> *Nokoru kumanaku*
> *sumeru yo no tsuki*

すめるよのつき
澄める夜の月

の残こるくまなく

あはれさへ(え)

あはぢの(淡路)しまの(島)

あはれと(れ)みる見る

あ は(わ) と み る (5 syllables)

a   *wa*   *to*   *mi*   *ru*

foam   as when   see

あ は(わ) ぢ の し ま の (7 syllables)

A   *wa*   *ji*   *no*   *shi*   *ma*   *no*

place name (possessive) island (possessive)

あ は(わ) れ さ へ(え) (5 syllables)

a   *wa*   *re*   *sa*   *e*

pathos   even

の こ る く ま な く (7 syllables)

no   *ko*   *ru*   *ku*   *ma*   *na*   *ku*

remain   in every corner

す め る よ の つ き (7 syllables)

su   *me*   *ru*   *yo*   *no*   *tsuki*

clear   night (poss.) moon

Oh, foam-flecked island that wast nothing to me,
even such sorrow as mine is, on this night of
flawless beauty thou hast power to heal.

WALEY[11]

Awaji: in your name is all my sadness,
And clear you stand in the light of the moon
tonight.   SEIDENSTICKER[12]

As Seidensticker's note informs us, there is a three-way *kake-kotoba* with the word *awa*, "foam," touching the name of the island, Awaji, and the sentiment, *aware*. Here is also an allusion to the *Shinkokinshū* poem number 1513:

> Awaji in the moonlight, like distant foam:
> From these cloudy sovereign heights it seems
> so near.   SEIDENSTICKER[13]

For Genji the foam is no longer distant. Remembering that *Shinkokinshū* poem, but seeing the cloudlessness of this night by contrast, Genji is painfully but sweetly reminded that he is now banished from the court.

In all things, therefore, a sensitivity to the delicacy and subtlety of beauty was most admired. Not only was a courtier expected to compose delicate poetry, but the way each poem was written, the shading of the ink, the selection of the paper, and more were also meticulously scrutinized for evidence of courtly sensibility.

Western readers often wonder in what respect Genji could be the object of so much admiration, not only in the novel itself, but as an idealized character throughout the history of Japanese literature. We must look for the answer not in our own concepts of heroic action, nor even in existing Japanese codes of stoic nobility, but in the Heian ideals of aristocratic sensibility, of which Genji is the quintessential manifestation.

IV

Biography of Murasaki Shikibu

Murasaki Shikibu, or Lady Murasaki as she is normally called in English, was the daughter of Fujiwara Tametoki, a scholar of Chinese who was assigned to the Board of Rites (Shikibu), and who belonged to one of the weaker cadet branches of the powerful Fujiwara clan described earlier.

The year of her birth is usually given as A.D. 978, though it may have been as early as 973. She did have an older sister, and her brother, Nobunori, was most likely born the year after she was. In that same year, her mother died, probably in childbirth.

Marrying again, their father had three more children: a daughter; a son, who later became Governor of Hitachi; and another son, who became a Buddhist priest. Of all these, it seems Lady Murasaki grew up on closest terms with her elder sister, who might have served as the prototype for the character of Agemaki (Ōigimi in Seidensticker), for she also died in her early twenties, leaving her sister to feel very much alone in the world.

Shortly after the death of her beloved sister, Murasaki accompanied her father on his assignment to Echizen (present-day Fukui Province), perhaps trying to leave her grief behind. A year later, though, she returned to Kyōto alone, where she met the amorous Fujiwara Nobutaka. Despite his advanced age, he ardently courted Lady Murasaki and in 999 married her.

In the year 1000, Murasaki gave birth to a daughter who was to be her only child, for in 1001 her husband died, and Murasaki was for the third time in her short life prematurely bereft of an intimate relationship.

About this time she probably began writing *The Tale of Genji*. There are many legends, mostly apocryphal, describing this event. Most popularly it is believed she retired in her grief to Ishiyama Temple, where one cloudless night beneath the full moon she began writing the "Suma" and "Akashi" chapters (12 and 13). Though this romantic account is very popular, especially among the monks at Ishiyama Temple, the more mundane story also persists that, in the service that she subsequently entered as an attendant upon the youthful Empress Akiko, she was challenged to come up with something more entertaining than the existing tales of such things as supernatural maidens from heaven, tales which were by then all so well known as to be boring.

One thing that does seem to be sure is that many of the anecdotes and characters in *The Tale of Genji* were drawn from Lady Murasaki's scrupulous observations of life at court. For example, Akiko (Shōshi), in whose service Murasaki was employed, was the younger of two rival imperial consorts and lived in the Fujitsubo apartments of the palace; and her jealous rival, Empress Sadako (Teishi), in whose service was Murasaki's most notorious literary rival, Sei Shōnagon, had lived in the Kokiden apartments (see p. 179). This parallels the sort of conflict that exists in the novel between the two characters named after those apartments. Many characters and events described in *Murasaki Shikibu Nikki* (Lady Murasaki's Diary) have curious parallels in the novel as well.

Conversely, her name, Murasaki, which means purple or lavender, was apparently bestowed because of the popularity of her novel at court. As seen in this quote from her diary, she was dubbed Murasaki after Genji's favorite wife and the romantic heroine through most of the novel:

> The First Officer of the Light Bodyguard said, "I think Lady Murasaki must be here." I listened, thinking. "How can she be here in a place where there is no such graceful person as Prince Genji?"[1]

From her diary we also learn as much as we know about her personality. She describes, for instance, how as a child she was particularly quick with her lessons, outshining her brother and learning Chinese by eavesdropping on his lessons. Owing to the strong Confucian prejudice against women, she was, of course, excluded from any formal study of the Chinese classics. But, as a daughter of a court scholar, Lady Murasaki managed, after all, to learn considerably more than was expected or thought proper for a woman. Yet there is a suggestion in her diary that this very eccentricity endeared her to Empress Akiko.

At any rate, Lady Murasaki seems to have been generally a lonely person who was not well liked by the throng of her contemporaries. She describes herself as follows:

> I wish I could be more adaptable and live more gaily in the present world—had I not an extraordinary sorrow—but whenever I hear delightful or interesting things, my yearning for a religious life grows stronger. I become melancholy and lament. I try to forget, for sorrow is vain. Am I too sinful?[2]

> Pretty and coy, shrinking from sight, unsociable, proud, fond of romance, vain and poetic, looking down upon others with a jealous eye—such is the opinion of those who do not know me, but after seeing me they say, "You are wonderfully gentle to meet with; I cannot identify you with that imagined one."
>
> I see that I have been slighted, hated, and looked down upon as an old gossip, and I must bear it, for it is my destiny to be solitary. The Queen said once, "You were ever mindful not to show your soul, but I have become more intimate with you than others."[3]

Beyond these self-reproaches, there is little to add except that her talent and name have long outlived the petty gossips who were her detractors, as well as the pompous male officialdom that widowed and isolated her. Ironically, it is only through her gentle, distaff spirit that the whole world of the Heian court can come so vividly to life again.

V

The Translations

There are three, or rather two and a half, translations of *The Tale of Genji* into English. The first, which is less than half of the total work, is the only one done by a native Japanese scholar, Baron Suematsu. As the oldest attempt, published at the turn of the century, it has historical value, but little else, and cannot be seriously discussed when comparing translations. It is brief to the extreme and tends to leave out difficult or questionable passages. Furthermore, though the English is meticulous, it lacks a sense of connotation, which kills much of the essence of this epic work.

Arthur Waley's translation is the most traditional and well-known version; at least it was from 1933 through 1976. It is available in a complete edition in the "Modern Library" series, but was originally published individually in six parts. The first part, consisting of the first nine chapters, is available in paperback through Doubleday–Anchor. Waley's famous comment that "so much is inevitably lost in translating Oriental literature that one must give a great deal in return"[1] suggests the direction his work took. He translated fast and free (some would say loose) in a manner described by Donald Keene as follows:

> He would read a passage over until he understood its meaning; then, without looking back at the passage, he wrote out an English assimilation. He would later consult the original again. If the content of the translation was the same, he would let it pass, even if some words had been added or deleted.[2]

It can certainly be argued that the differences between Japanese of the Heian period and modern English are so dramatic that such a method is understandable.

Edward Seidensticker's newest translation of the entire work has set out to correct Waley. There are several passages, and in one case an entire chapter, that Waley had not translated, as well as a number of passages that are inaccurate in his translation. Seidensticker, in general, has tried to create a closer approximation to Murasaki Shikibu's style, or what that style might be in English. Happily, he has seen fit to paragraph more mercifully than Waley, and he has also more conveniently and consistently set off and fastidiously annotated the many poems in the text, using a two-line, or couplet, formula to render the thirty-one syllable *waka,* where Waley just ran the poem on into the prose text.

Edwin Cranston's fine review of this new translation points out that Seidensticker may, however, have missed the mark in trying to capture Murasaki's sense of rhythm. Seidensticker's sentence structures, for example, do not seem to be as complex ("labyrinthine") as the original, whereas Waley's are. His regular couplet formula for all the poems may be doing injustice to the original five-line, asymmetrical *waka*.[3]

Yet, this new translation does preserve more of the ambiguity or vagueness of the original by providing fewer clues as to the identity of speakers in dialogue and by frequently referring to characters, as the original does, by their rank or relationship to other characters, instead of by contriving set names for them as Waley had done.

For the most part, Waley tried to create a viable novel in English, and he tended to sacrifice uniquely Japanese aspects of the story that he felt could not after all be grasped by the Occidental reader. Beyond the stylistic features, he also tended to translate out that amorphous and subtle Heian aesthetic, *mono no aware,* which Seidensticker was much more careful to preserve. Instead of trying to capture this Heian sensitivity to the inherent pathos of all that is beautiful, he seems to have rendered it as a British romantic, or worse, pastoral attitude, devoid of the religious-poetic impact it should have. The reader might want to compare the passage in the chapter "Yūgiri" in Waley on page 715, and in Seidensticker on page 695, which begins, "It was (about) the middle of the Ninth Month. . . ."

This is not to say that Waley's translation is easier or less confusing than Seidensticker's. Seidensticker, for instance, makes a greater effort to explain the relationship between each chapter and its title, and, as Seidensticker points out in his introduction, in spite of the fact that Waley made many inexplicable cuts, his translation is also marked by "the process of amplifying and embroidering." It seems, in fact, that word for word Waley gave even more than he lost, for Seidensticker's translation, with more of the original represented, is still shorter than the Waley translation.

For further information and a more detailed discussion of the differences between the two translations, the reader is referred to Earl Miner's review in *The Times Literary Supplement;* Katsuhiko Takeda's review in the *Japan Quarterly;* Edwin Cranston's review in the *Journal of Japanese Studies;* and Marian Ury's article in the *Harvard Journal of Asiatic Studies.* There is also a very interesting comparison by Marian Ury of the Waley English translation with the Benl German translation in the *Journal of Japanese Studies.* Full details of all these articles can be found in the Bibliography (p. 185).

PART TWO

The Tale of Genji

VI

Detailed Chapter Précis and Commentaries of Chapters 1—9

In sections VI and VII, the Japanese chapter title before each summary is usually followed by one or two translations. Where two versions are given, the first is Waley's and the second, Seidensticker's. One English title may suggest that the two translations concur, or that either translator adopts the Japanese title. Consult Japanese Chapter Titles with Translations, page 7, to determine the title used by each translator.

Not only do Waley and Seidensticker differ in their choice of names for many characters, they also occasionally ascribe the same name to different characters. Further, one translator may name a character unnamed by the other. To minimize these difficulties (without being forced to choose either translation as primary) the names used in the two sections are those considered least confusing, or those felt to be closest to the original. The alternative, if any, is given in parentheses the first time the name appears in each summary. ''S.'' within the parentheses stands for Seidensticker's translation, and ''W.'' for Waley's.

桐
壺 *1 · KIRITSUBO*

The Paulownia Court
(From Genji's birth to his 12th year)

There is a lady, Kiritsubo, who is the emperor's favorite, but who has no strong family backing at court. She suffers greatly from the insults of jealous competitors, but is not capable of defending herself. She bears a beautiful son, who is so magnificent he is a possible rival to the title of crown prince, which was already understood to belong to the emperor's eldest son. The jealousy and ill will heighten. The boy grows more beautiful and favored, but his mother becomes ill and dies. So the child goes off with his grandmother. Meanwhile, the emperor is abject in his mourning and writes letters begging for the child, at least, to be sent to him. After a time the boy does return, but shortly thereafter his grandmother also dies and, now six, he mourns as well. Korean ambassadors come, and Genji's life of distinction is predicted.

Owing to his mother's weak position, when the time comes, the boy is not made crown prince, but is initiated into the court and assigned membership in the non-royal Gen clan (hence his name, Genji). The eldest son of the emperor and Lady Kokiden is after all made crown prince. And the emperor takes a new mistress, Fujitsubo, resembling Genji's mother, but with better family connections. At the end of the chapter Genji is married off to the Minister of the Left's daughter, Princess Aoi.

*

COMMENTARY: The chief function of this chapter is obviously to introduce the main character, Genji. This is done in a very Heian way, *ab ovo,* by describing his parents, particularly his mother, as the emperor needs little introduction. The story is set not in the distant past as was the custom, but in a vague past which resembled the present for Murasaki's readers. Genji's mother is beautiful and cursed by jealousy. She is therefore the very embodiment of what has been called *aware* (see p. 42).

Genji is likewise handsome in the extreme, possessing a beauty and sensibility of a bygone era, not really in keeping with the decadent present; hence is he dubbed Hikaru Genji, "the shining Genji."

As Waley points out, in many respects this chapter is still influenced by the previous traditions: the use of the Korean fortune-teller, the references to Chinese emperors, and other tricks are after all understandable in these first chapters. Murasaki soon enough comes into her own. Many believe this chapter was written after the other chapters to fill out the ancestral details of the by then popular Genji.

Kiri (paulownia) design.

帚
木　*2 · HAHAKIGI*

The Broom Tree
(Summer of Genji's 17th year)

At his wife's estate Genji develops a friendship with his brother-in-law, Tō-no-Chūjō. As young gallants, they have each had some experience in pursuing affairs, and one rainy night at Genji's palace they compare notes. Tō-no-Chūjō presents three rather rigid categories of women according to social class (for historical background, see p. 25), and Genji is challenging him, when they are joined by friends. Uma-no-kami (in S., "a guards officer") tries to accommodate the system to Genji's criticism and offhandedly suggests that there may be a beautiful unknown woman hidden away somewhere because her family has fallen upon hard times. Genji then falls into a deep sleep, while his friends discuss several types of women, all of whom he shall encounter as the story progresses.

As Genji wakes, Uma-no-kami tells the story of a jealous lover who bit his finger. He then tells another story of an unsatisfactory lover, a lute player, who was playing the field as well. Chūjō next tells the story of a lover (we learn later to be Yūgao) who bore him a daughter, but lost out by being too meek and forgiving. Finally, Shikibu, a young man from the Ministry of Rites, is forced to tell a story, so he tells them of a lady who was too erudite (in W., "a bluestocking") and therefore too masculine, preferring Chinese to Japanese expressions. She put him off, one evening when he called, with her breath smelling of garlic she had taken medicinally. They all conclude, rather characteristically, that the perfect woman should be loyal and cultured, but passive and, when appropriate, willing to feign ignorance to flatter her suitor.

The chapter then takes a new turn as Genji goes to visit his wife, Aoi, at Sanjō. She is cold and curt with him, similar to Uma-no-kami's jealous lover without the histrionics. Genji is prevented from returning directly home by various religious portents, so he is invited to Kii-no-kami's house.

Kii-no-kami's father has married a young lady whom Genji overhears talking; the discussion seems to be about Genji himself. Genji also meets an attractive young boy, her brother and Kii-no-kami's stepuncle (later named Kogimi). After everyone is asleep, Genji breaks into the lady's apartment and carries her off to his room "in a dreamlike encounter." Leaving the next day, Genji takes the young boy into his service as a page and uses him as a messenger. The boy carries letters back and forth, but the young lady does not encourage Genji's suit. He contrives to visit her again, but she refuses him. He responds with a poem about the inhospitable broom tree, and is left to sleep with the boy instead.

*

COMMENTARY: This chapter may be considered in two parts. The first part is the famous "Amayo no Shinasadame"

(Appraisement of Women on a Rainy Night). Though these first three chapters are considered Murasaki's most juvenile and derivative, this scene is indeed admirable by virtue of the attitude the court lady is able to sustain as she looks at herself and her peers from a masculine point of view. Not only that, but each character in the discussion does emerge as a distinct personality and, most of all, Genji's sensitivity and openmindedness are seen by comparison.

This scene has further been regarded as the key to the structure of the whole novel. Certainly, reading it over after completing the first nine chapters reveals previews of most of the major people seen; but it is not that straight-forward. It is just as easy to see several women entering one of the anecdotes; for example, the jealous lover prefigures Rokujō as well as Aoi. Also, Fujitsubo's importance is not really forecast.

If not a key to structure, the scene does provide Genji and his companions with some stereotypes that may be explored in the rest of the Tale. This scene will be frequently referred to in later chapters. Genji's part in it, including the period he was asleep, should be studied closely.

The second scene (and the title of the whole chapter as well) seems really to belong to Chapter 3, "Utsusemi," for it is essentially the first part of the story about her. The titles of both Chapters 2 and 3 refer to the one lady. Why did Murasaki include this with the rainy night conversation? Perhaps she did not want that first scene to attract too much attention. Perhaps she was carried away in a fit of writing. Or perhaps she wanted no break between the night of theorizing and Genji's actual experience, which was not what he expected.

Another possible link between the two scenes may be established by looking at the way the chapter opens and the way it closes. Genji is disappointed by his wife, Aoi, in the beginning and turns to Tō-no-Chūjō, her brother, for masculine comfort. At the end of the chapter, Genji is disappointed by Utsusemi (as Waley begins to call her in Chapter 3) and turns to her brother, the young boy, for comfort. Murasaki, therefore, might be making a statement about masculine loyalties and friendships as they compare to heterosexual relationships.

空
蟬 *3 · UTSUSEMI*

The Shell of the Locust
(Summer of Genji's 17th year)

Smarting from the rejection, Genji is unwilling to give up his suit for Utsusemi (in S., ''the lady of the locust shell''). Even the young boy, her brother, sympathizes with Genji and resolves to help him try again.

In plain clothes, Genji follows the boy into her apartments. She is playing the game of Go, a kind of chess, with a vivacious companion, Nokiba-no-ogi. Genji is able to spy on them as it is hot and various shutters are open to catch any summer breeze. The game finished, Genji prepares to break in on Utsusemi, but she catches the scent of his robes and flees, leaving one of her outer robes behind. Genji mistakenly breaks in on her companion instead. He pretends it was she he was calling on and makes the best of it before leaving. He only narrowly escapes detection by a maid and returns home sulking. There he writes the poem comparing Utsusemi's robe to a cicada husk *(utsusemi)*, after which she is named. The lady herself is upset and wishes Genji would leave her alone.

*

COMMENTARY: It is interesting to see how the lady of this chapter is referred to as Utsusemi even before the incident by which Genji gives her that name. In this, Genji's first recorded encounter, there are several points being made. First, after the very chauvinistic remarks of the rainy night conversation, Genji is shown how men can be hurt by women as well. Secondly, there is the contrast between Utsusemi who is not actually so beautiful, and her companion who is too vivacious, which Genji sees as superficial. Genji is obviously more attracted by the quiet and sullen temperament of Utsusemi, which he sees as subtle and fraught with sensitivity, than he is by the greater physical beauty of Nokiba-no-ogi.

The second amusing feature of this chapter is the sympathy of the young boy, who is more concerned with Genji's feelings than with his own sister's. He actually goes out of his way to compromise his sister's virtue. A deep gulf seems to exist between masculine and feminine interests; a gulf not even family ties can bridge.

夕
顔 *4 · YŪGAO*

Evening Faces
(Summer to the 10th month of Genji's 17th year)

On his way to visit Lady Rokujō, Genji learns that his old nursemaid, who has since become a Buddhist nun, is sick and may be near death, so he goes to visit her with her natural son, Koremitsu. At a nearby house, they are admiring the beautiful flowers called *yūgao* or "evening faces," when a little girl comes out with a scented white fan for Genji to take a flower on.

They then go in to visit the nun, and she shows an even greater attachment to Genji than to her own son. On his way out, Genji's curiosity is aroused by the possibility of hidden delights in the house of *yūgao,* so he dispatches Koremitsu to investigate, who reports that Tō-no-Chūjō had been there and that a lady evidently resided therein. Genji cannot resist, so he disguises himself and arranges a clandestine meeting through her maid, Ukon.

Yūgao is a very frail, submissive beauty, and Genji

Yūgao (evening face) design.

quickly associates her with Tō-no-Chūjō's rainy night story. Unlike Tō-no-Chūjō, however, Genji is attracted by this gentility. In fact, he resolves to take her away. Unable to resist and very frightened, Yūgao is rushed off with Ukon to a deserted hideaway.

That night, Genji dreams of a jealous lady resembling Rokujō, and when he wakes up, he sees an apparition by Yūgao's pillow. He tries to wake her, but she is no longer breathing. Genji panics, wakes Ukon and Koremitsu, but it is too late; Yūgao is dead. Koremitsu sends Genji back to his palace at Nijō and takes her body to a nunnery in the eastern hills for funeral rites.

At Nijō, Genji is distracted and cannot rest. He cannot appear at court as he has been polluted by death (see p. 37 on Japanese religion) and he cannot calm himself, so he sets out on horseback with Koremitsu to see Yūgao's body one last time. Returning, Genji sickens and falls off his horse. The illness persists for a long time. When he finally recovers, he summons Ukon and confirms that Yūgao was, in fact, Tō-no-Chūjō's mistress. Genji decides to retain Ukon out of sympathy and asks her to find Yūgao's daughter by Tō-no-Chūjō, whom Genji plans to raise under his protection.

The chapter ends with a last poetic exchange with Utsusemi (in S., "the lady of the locust shell"), whom he also loses, and with her stepdaughter and companion at chess, Nokiba-no-ogi. There is also an interesting author apology at the end of the chapter for going into all this scandalous behavior.

COMMENTARY: This chapter is named after a flower associated with the frail beauty referred to in Chapter 2 by Tō-no-Chūjō as a lady who seemed impossible of jealousy; but this chapter is also about Lady Rokujō, for whom, especially in the matter of jealousy, Yūgao is a foil. Though Rokujō is introduced in this chapter, she is, from the first, referred to as if she had already been presented. This seems to be a convention that Murasaki Shikibu often used, though it may indicate that some earlier chapters have been lost.

Rokujō is an older woman whom Genji pursued but has begun to lose interest in now that she has surrendered. It is remarked how much Genji seems to enjoy surmounting difficulties.

Another interesting feature of this chapter is the sense of pity or sympathy that dominates Genji's character as well as the mood of the entire Tale. It is sympathy for his nurse that interrupts his route to Rokujō and starts the Yūgao episode. And it is sympathy for her weakness and vulnerability that attracts Genji to her and strengthens his affection. Yūgao is the first of a group of lovers that we may associate with Kiritsubo, his mother. Remember, it was jealousy that killed Kiritsubo, just as it was the jealousy of Tō-no-Chūjō's wife that originally affected Yūgao, and Rokujō's jealousy that eventually kills her.

The figure of the jealous female becomes an archetype in classic Japanese literature. The *hannya,* as it is called, is the most fearsome of the Japanese mythic demons, reminiscent of the Western saw, ''Hell hath no fury as a woman scorned.'' It must be noted that, while it is often called Rokujō's ghost, it is not a ghost in the Western meaning.

Hannya.

Rokujō herself is not dead. She is not even necessarily aware of what she is doing. Instead, we should see this (as Waley tells us in a footnote in a later chapter) as indicative of a basic theme of the novel: that hate can kill.[1]

Collating the notes of Ivan Morris and Sen'ichi Hisamatsu, it is possible to establish Genji's age in Chapters 2, 3, and 4 as seventeen. This would make Rokujō twenty-five; Fujitsubo, twenty-two; Aoi, twenty-one; and Yūgao, about nineteen. These calculations, however, do not exactly correspond to Waley's reckoning.

若
紫 *5 · WAKA MURASAKI*

Lavender
(3rd to 10th month of Genji's 18th year)

Genji is sick and is persuaded to seek help from a
holy man living in a cave in the northern hills. He goes
there incognito and receives treatment from the reclusive sage. While recuperating, he is humored by
his attendants with the story of a certain Governor
of Akashi in Harima who became a lay priest and retired there with his daughter, whom he expected to
raise to a higher rank in life than he had managed for
himself.

Genji must wait an extra day or so for his convales-
cence, so in the evening he wanders to a nearby house
where he catches a glimpse of a beautiful, young girl
(about ten years old). She quaintly reminds him of
Fujitsubo, the current favorite of his father, the emperor. The priest from this villa invites Genji to visit,
during the course of which the child, Murasaki, is
revealed to be Fujitsubo's niece. Genji is overcome (insomuch as he already has a crush on Fujitsubo) and seeks
to adopt the child; but he is not taken seriously.
Everyone thinks that Genji is after a fresh mistress
and that he has somehow misunderstood her true age.

His cure complete, Genji is about to leave. He asks
again to adopt Murasaki and is again refused. Suddenly,
Tō-no-Chūjō and some other friends from the court

Fuji (wisteria) design.

arrive to accompany him. They first picnic by a stream and play music together.

Back at court, Genji is picked up by his father-in-law and brought to visit Aoi. He tries to talk to her, but she is cold and unreceptive. Genji sleeps and dreams of the little girl. The next day Genji presses his suit for Murasaki by letter and is again refused. About this time Fujitsubo falls ill and is away from court. Genji takes this opportunity to arrange, via her maid, Ōmyōbu, a secret visit and spends the night. Fujitsubo becomes pregnant, and the emperor, unaware of Genji's role in this, regularly summons both of them to his presence, much to their discomfort.

Meanwhile, the little girl is finally made available to Genji for adoption since her grandmother, the nun who was taking care of her, dies. Genji hurries to be with the girl and commence adoption proceedings, but her father, Prince Hyōbu (in W., Hyōbukyō), also decides to take charge of her. Genji hears of this at Aoi's residence and immediately goes to fetch (kidnap) her, lying to her nurse, Shōnagon. At his Nijō palace, Genji begins her "education," and the chapter ends on a happy note.

COMMENTARY: As indicated, this chapter is actually titled ''Waka Murasaki'' or ''Young Murasaki.'' *Murasaki* is the color purple or lavender, suggesting the color of the wisteria *(fuji)* which shows her relationship in Genji's mind to Lady Fujitsubo.

Genji's illness at the beginning of the chapter is given as an ague by Waley and as malaria by Seidensticker, but in either case the probable intention was for us to connect this physical illness to Genji's emotional depression after the death of Yūgao. The old sage on the mountain who effects a cure is more of an exorcist than a physician, and it is his incantations that appear to have an effect on the disease.

The affair with young Murasaki in this chapter parallels, and is emotionally and thematically combined with, Genji's affair with Fujitsubo. This affair is, in many respects, an oedipal relationship insomuch as Genji equates Fujitsubo with his own mother, Kiritsubo. Both were of unrivaled beauty in their respective courts, and both, as consorts especially favored by the emperor, were objects of jealous plots. Of course, Fujitsubo has greater family connections that enable her to endure better, but surely in Genji's mind they are associated. Similarly, little Murasaki suffers from the jealousy of her wicked stepmother in an almost Cinderella-like fashion.

末
摘
花 *6 · SUETSUMU HANA*

The Saffron Flower/The Safflower
(Genji's 18th year, beginning to end)

While all this is going on, Genji is still fondly but
sadly remembering his affairs with Yūgao and Utsusemi. One day, Tayū (in W., Myōbu) tells him of
a certain orphaned princess who is reputed to be an
excellent *koto* player. This arouses Genji's curiosity
and sympathy, so he resolves to visit her and hear her
play. Secretly he contrives to do so one evening, but
Tō-no-Chūjō follows. They then agree to become
friendly rivals for her favor. Neither is at first
successful, though Genji insinuates he is. He talks to
Tayū as go-between and protests that he is serious,
though it is evident he is not.

One day, then, Tayū arranges for Genji to secretly
visit her, but the princess is flustered by his appearance and is incapable of deciding anything. It is left
for a precocious attendant, Jijū, to make reply to
Genji for her and save the day. Then Genji manages
a quick glimpse and is not impressed, so he leaves
somewhat disillusioned. Poems are exchanged on the
following day as prescribed, and Tayū pleads with him
to visit her again, which he does out of pity. This time,
though, he gets an even better look at her and sees she
has a big, red-tipped nose which he cruelly likens to

an icicle in a parting poem. Again, out of a sense of pity, he sends her gifts, but is struck by her poor behavior for someone of her rank. .

Tayū subsequently brings a gift from the princess to Genji: a poorly made Chinese jacket with a very inelegant poem, obviously written without help. Genji writes a return poem in which he compares her unhappily to a safflower. At the end of the chapter, he returns to his palace at Nijō and teases Murasaki by painting his own nose red.

*

COMMENTARY: In this chapter, Genji is once again attracted by the possibility of a mysterious lover of high birth and poor condition. This time, though, we see Genji at his most careless and adolescent. He is playing a game with the princess' feelings.

The princess herself is used as a multiple foil to Yūgao, Utsusemi, and Murasaki. She is of the highest rank, but inarticulate, old-fashioned, and totally lacking in elegance and feminine grace. Again we see the association of Chinese things with the masculine and the formal. To Genji's credit, we also see his sympathy for the princess, which is perhaps an extension of the sympathy and pity Genji feels for himself and Murasaki.

There is an interesting question raised: Is Genji (and are the values of the court) too superficial and concerned too much with the physical? Note the last scene with Murasaki which acts as an envoy to the whole.

The fact that the events in this chapter take place concurrently with those in the last chapter is curious. It might be part of a deliberate style, or, as Seidensticker suggests, this chapter might have been written after the others were already in circulation. Impossible to recall finished work for rewriting, the chapter might have been composed as an overlay.

The princess is compared to the safflower because it apparently has a brilliant red blossom.

紅
葉
賀   7 · *MOMIJI NO GA*

The Festival of Red Leaves/An Autumn Excursion
(Autumn of Genji's 18th year to the fall of his 19th)

The emperor plans a royal festival and holds a special rehearsal for Fujitsubo, whose pregnancy is now advanced. Tō-no-Chūjō and Genji dance a Bugaku called "The Waves of the Blue Sea" *(Seigaiha)*, and Genji's performance is so magnificent that he attracts the great praise of the emperor and greater jealousy and malice from Lady Kokiden who, of course, sees Genji as a threat to her son, the crown prince.

Genji tries to visit his wife, Lady Aoi, at Sanjō, but she is very upset with him. She has heard of his keeping another lady, namely Murasaki, at his home and remains stiff and aloof in his presence. Genji is put off by her "perfection" and does not stay long. His father-in-law, however, is still fond of him and gives him a precious belt as he leaves.

Murasaki is still very young, but is starting to mature in manners and appearance. As the New Year approaches, Fujitsubo grows more and more feeble. She finally gives birth to a son, and there is much rejoicing, though everyone cannot help noticing how much the baby resembles Genji.

Murasaki begins to demand more and more of Genji's time, yet there are many ladies at court hoping for an affair with him. A humorous incident ensues when one such lady in her fifties (in S., Naishi) makes a pass at him one day. Genji is embarrassed and tries not to hurt her feelings, but when Tō-no-Chūjō bursts in on them, a mock battle is staged at the lady's expense. Genji is shown, therefore, to have a wild side to his character.

At the end of this chapter, the emperor surprises everyone by proclaiming Fujitsubo as his empress (instead of the heir apparent's mother, Kokiden) and her son (and Genji's) as the crown prince to succeed Kokiden's son as emperor.

*

COMMENTARY: This chapter shows us more of Genji's personality. The dance he performs is so wonderful even his enemies are forced to admit that his talent and beauty are extraordinary. The point is constantly made that Genji seems to be too good for this world, as if he belonged to an earlier age of a more rarified elegance. The ideals of delicacy and refinement are continuously extolled in this chapter; what Ivan Morris describes as the "Cult of Beauty."

Murasaki is being specially educated to appreciate Genji's capacities and she is seen in contrast to Aoi (Genji's wife) who, though perfect in so many ways, does not appreciate him. Thus, there is a conflict between Aoi's almost Confucian propriety and the Heian aesthetic sensitivity. So far only Fujitsubo, now raised completely out of his reach, seems truly capable of appreciating his shining perfection. It should be realized, of course, that this is a perfection of artistic sensibility and not of personality development or maturity.

The affair with the old lady does seem to be a distraction, though it might be called comic relief. Seidensticker in his journal remarks:

> One feels that such stories are there because they are based on actual happenings and because Murasaki's imagination has momentarily faltered; and one is reminded of the *Tales of Ise* and feels that Murasaki has not yet advanced a great distance from its world.[2]

There are, no doubt, many incidents in the Tale based on actual events of Murasaki's day. Whether they distract or contribute to the structural flow is difficult to assess. They may even be said to add a sparkle of social satire.

花
宴 *8 · HANA NO EN*

The Flower Feast/The Festival of the Cherry Blossoms
(Spring of Genji's 20th year)

Like the last chapter, this one begins with a royal feast. It is in honor of Empress Fujitsubo and the new crown prince. At this banquet the emperor convenes a Chinese poetry contest in which contestants are given words to begin their poems. As before, Genji acquits himself magnificently, though Tō-no-Chūjō also puts in a good showing.

After the feast, Genji is prowling about hoping to gain access to Fujitsubo's chambers. Unable to do so, he does manage to gain admittance to Lady Kokiden's apartments and finds therein an entrancing lady, humming the song, "Oborozukiyo" (Misty Moon of Spring). She is quickly seduced, but refuses to reveal her identity, and so she is known by that song title. He calculates that she is one of Kokiden's sisters and, as he suspects, she turns out to be the sixth, who is engaged to be married to the heir apparent. Before parting in the darkness, she and Genji exchange fans.

Later that spring, Oborozukiyo's father holds a wisteria feast, inviting Genji. Dressed precociously, Genji attends and, in the less formal setting of this party, sets out looking for Oborozukiyo singing a song about a fan. In this manner he identifies her, and they exchange poems.

*

COMMENTARY: Here there is a connection asserted between Fujitsubo and Oborozukiyo. Not unlike the last chapter, the first point made is the superior nature of Genji's accomplishments. Note in both chapters how Genji's efforts are always seen as better than those of the professional but lowborn artists.

The episode with Oborozukiyo sets a new plot in motion. Genji has been reckless, but now he seems to be going too far. He has already presumed to seduce the present emperor's consort; now he has defiled the future emperor's wife and sister of his greatest enemy, Kokiden. Both translations end with the ominous line: "He was delighted, and yet . . ." The events of this chapter will often be recollected in later chapters as the high-water mark of Genji's carefree youth.

葵 *9 · AOI*

Heartvine
(4th month of Genji's 22nd year to the New Year's of his 23rd)

As the chapter opens, it is clear that Genji's father, the emperor, has abdicated. The new emperor (Suzaku) is Genji's brother, son of Lady Kokiden. Of course, the old emperor will still have the lion's share of power and will establish his own court in retirement.

We learn that Rokujō used to be married to Prince Zembō, a brother of the old emperor; a brother who

Aoi (heartvine) design.

would have become emperor himself had he lived.
Their daughter is to be a high priestess at Ise (Shintō)
Shrine. Genji is rebuked by his father for his poor
treatment of Rokujō. But now his own wife, Lady
Aoi, is pregnant, and so he finds himself with even
less time to spend on Rokujō.

A ceremony of lustration for the Kamo River festival
is held, and everyone turns out to see Genji. The
streets are packed with carriages. Lady Aoi herself only
decides to attend at the last minute. At the festival her
men have to push their way into a decent vantage,
seriously damaging the pride and position of another
carriage, which turns out to be Lady Rokujō's.

Afterward, as Aoi's pregnancy progresses, her
health declines and it is suspected that she is the victim
of spiritual possession by Rokujō, who seems unaware
of her part in all this (but the growing evidence of
Rokujō's own dreams is hard for her to ignore). As the
time nears, Genji softens toward his wife, but, in
spite of all the circumstantial evidence, he cannot believe Rokujō is behind the illness. Once, however, as he
is attending Aoi, he hears Rokujō's voice and is startled.
Soon thereafter a baby boy is born (to be called Yūgiri)

and everyone relaxes, but after a few days the possession strikes again and Lady Aoi dies. Genji mourns profusely with the whole court.

When some of the pain of this subsides, Genji's interests turn to young Murasaki. He decides the time is ripe to take her as his wife. (She would be about fifteen years old.) Murasaki is, of course, unaware of his designs and is shocked when he forces himself on her. Koremitsu conspires with Genji to arrange a secret marriage, and the plan is consummated, though Murasaki is far from happy about it.

As the chapter ends, Genji and others begin to notice the uncomfortable resemblance between Aoi's son and Fujitsubo's, but no one makes the connection.

*

COMMENTARY: This chapter is parallel in many respects to Chapter 6, "Yūgao." From the very beginning Rokujō is a central figure and shares the stage of events with Aoi. The old emperor's reprimand of Genji indicates the direction of the plot. It seems that Genji's fickleness and improprieties are at last catching up with him. It is sad that Aoi, who has been most angry with Genji for his behavior, should in the end be the one who pays with her life for it. Perhaps the famous scene of the "carriage quarrel" (kuruma-arasoi) is intended in some way to offset Genji's responsibility and to make Aoi at least partially responsible for her own demise. In any event, guilt is made to weigh heavily on Genji and shall have a maturing, if not reforming, effect on him. It is very interesting that little or no guilt is placed on Rokujō. Note also that, as in the case of Kiritsubo at the time of Genji's birth, Aoi does not die till at least some brief time after she delivers, for as Seidensticker informs us, the Heian Japanese believed it a great sin to die in childbirth.[3]

For an interesting discussion between Genji and Lady Murasaki in the twilight of their lives, looking back at this incident, see "Fuji no Uraba" (Wisteria Leaves)[4] and the second "Wakana" (New Herbs) chapter.[5]

A partial explanation for some of Genji's caprice is given when the authoress comments:

> It is in general the unexplored that attracts us, and Genji tended to fall most deeply in love with those who gave him least encouragement.   WALEY[6]

> We do not often find in this world that the actuality is better than the anticipation, but it was Genji's nature to be drawn to retiring women.
>   SEIDENSTICKER[7]

Genji's notorious sympathy and strong oedipal associations have already been mentioned. Adding to them this third feature, we begin to have a good picture of Genji's personality and the triad of his amorous instincts.

The abruptness with which he turns to Murasaki after the death of Aoi has often surprised readers. It seems possible to explain it only in terms of guilt consolation. He had made a bad husband to Aoi and was training Murasaki to be a perfect wife. With Aoi's death he seemed compelled to consummate a true marriage to make an "honest man" of himself, as it were, and assuage his guilt.

VII

Summaries of Chapters 10—54

賢
木   *10 · SAKAKI*

The Sacred Tree
(9th month of Genji's 23rd year to summer of his 25th year)

Lady Rokujō, somewhat distracted by jealousy and anxiety over Genji, decides to join her daughter as a Shintō priestess at Ise. Genji, of course, tries to talk her out of it, but with the death of his father (the emperor) power shifts to Lady Kokiden and the Minister of the Right. Genji's power and influence decline, and he seems to mature. He tries to rekindle his affair with Fujitsubo, but she, fearing for her son's position as crown prince, also forsakes Genji and the world to become a Buddhist nun. The chapter takes its name from the branches of the tree on which Genji ties love notes for Rokujō and Fujitsubo.

Genji tries to forget his sorrow by renewing acquaintances with Princess Asagao (also an illicit relationship) and Murasaki. At the end of the chapter he is recklessly pursuing his old flame Oborozukiyo, (currently the young emperor's consort) when he is caught in the act by the Minister of the Right, her father. Her sister, Kokiden, and he are now bent on Genji's debacle.

Tied love note.

花
散
里 *11 · HANACHIRU SATO*

The Village of Falling Flowers/The Orange Blossoms
(5th month, 20th day of Genji's 25th year)

This is a short chapter, sometimes considered with "Sakaki," in which Genji shows a better side of his personality. He has begun to think of Lady Reikeiden, who was a consort of his father's. Realizing that she and her sister are now cut off from the court and its privileges, Genji undertakes to visit and cheer them. On the way, he is sidetracked briefly by the house of an old flame. He sends Koremitsu in with a poem. Her reply pretends ignorance and he presses on. By contrast, at Lady Reikeiden's house Genji is warmly received and they happily talk of old times, such that it is concluded there are two types of women: the fickle and the constant. Lady Reikeiden and her sister are admiringly placed in the latter category.

須磨 *12 · SUMA*

Exile at Suma
(3rd month of Genji's 26th year to the 3rd month of his 27th)

Life is made more and more difficult for Genji in the capital, and with his fortunes thus declining he contemplates a self-imposed exile. This step, though, is not taken lightly as there are so many whom Genji loves, such as his young wife Murasaki, his infant son Yūgiri, Fujitsubo and their son, the crown prince, and even Oborozukiyo, the cause of his difficulty. Finally, however, Genji is forced to go to Suma, a lonely windswept shore, and submit himself to exile by powers Kokiden has marshaled against him. With a few loyal attendants he sails to Suma, where life is horribly rustic and void of all elegance. Partly to console himself and partly to occupy the time, he paints forlorn landscapes. While Genji is away, everyone grieves. Even the young emperor feels guilty that he betrayed his father's last wish to keep Genji by his side. But Kokiden prevails and forces everyone to stop sending messages to Genji. Only Tō-no-Chūjō and Genji's wife, Murasaki, manage to penetrate this ill will. Genji's loneliness and depression grow until his only desire is to end this exile and return to court.

明
石 *13 · AKASHI*

(3rd month of Genji's 27th year to the 8th month of his 28th)

The weather worsens and a severe storm wracks the coast for weeks on end. It is abnormally severe and people begin to fear for their lives. When the storm finally breaks, Genji has a dream of his dead father, the former emperor, who tells him to put out to sea immediately. Waking, Genji is visited by the ex-Governor of Harima who has just come miraculously over the sea to call on him. Genji had heard a story of him and his daughter earlier (in Chapter 5, ''Waka Murasaki''). Genji sets out with him and is likewise, by divine intervention, blown to Akashi where conditions are much more comfortable and like the capital. The former governor proceeds to foster an affair between his daughter and Genji in the hope of promoting her when Genji's exile is eventually lifted. The girl, however, is reticent and unwilling to throw herself at someone so elevated and refined. Genji is variously reminded by her of Aoi, Rokujō, and Fujitsubo. As he warms toward her, he starts to feel guilty about Murasaki pining for him in the capital. Meanwhile, in a dream the young emperor is visited by his father and begins to lean toward an official pardon of Genji. He is, of course, blocked by Kokiden, his mother, and they both grow ill as a result. Finally, he gains the upper hand and summons Genji back. Genji has just managed to consummate his affair with the lady at Akashi, however, so his good fortune is mixed with the regret of losing her.

澪
標 *14 · MIOTSUKUSHI*

The Flood Gauge/Channel Buoys
(10th month of Genji's 28th year to the 11th month of his 29th)

Genji's half brother, the emperor, at peace with his conscience, now abdicates the throne to Fujitsubo's (and secretly Genji's) son. Genji is restored at court and promoted while the Akashi lady has a baby girl. A fortune-teller had once said that his children would rise to royal greatness, and it all seems to be coming true. Genji regrets only that he let the girl be born inauspiciously in the provinces, but he plans to bring the girl to the capital soon and raise her properly. Genji then makes a pilgrimage to Akashi to thank the local god of Sumiyoshi for his divine aid in restoring his fortune. At the same time, the Akashi lady tries to make her own pilgrimage, but is so intimidated by Genji's display of wealth and magnificence, she retires. Genji hears of this and rushes to her boat writing poems about the channel buoys.

The chapter is then cut in two by a reminder of the condition of Lady Rokujō who has been ill and begs Genji to look after her beautiful daughter. Rokujō then dies abruptly, whereupon Genji persuades Regent Fujitsubo to list Rokujō's daughter as a consort for the new emperor (Genji's son), thereby preventing a less opportune affair between this daughter and the now-retired emperor.

蓬
生　*15 · YOMOGIU*

The Palace in the Tangled Woods/The Wormwood Patch
(Autumn of Genji's 28th year to the 4th month of his 29th)

This chapter refers back to the events of Chapter 6, "Suetsumu Hana." Since Genji paid court to the orphaned princess (in S., "the safflower princess"), she has been waiting patiently and faithfully for his return, while her own circumstances in the world have become worse and worse. The mansion she inherited from her father is in disrepair, but she cannot bear the thought of selling it. Slowly her friends and attendants, even Jijū, desert her and she is scorned by her less reputable relatives for being so stubborn. Genji is unaware of her condition until one evening, en route to another haunt, he chances to pass by her sadly deteriorated home and calls on her. He feels guilty for having left her so abjectly and resolves to take care of her and restore her fortune, even though, we are reminded, she is no great beauty.

關
屋 *16 · SEKIYA*

A Meeting at the Frontier/The Gatehouse
(Late fall to the 11th month of Genji's 29th year)

As the last chapter picked up the case of Suetsumu Hana (in S., ''the safflower princess''), this chapter refers to Utsusemi of Chapters 2 and 3. She had left with her husband for the provinces and only now is returning to the capital. As it happens, her procession and Genji's, which was on its own excursion, meet at the barrier gate to the frontier. Again Genji uses her brother, Kogimi, to deliver poetic entreaties, and her reply is, as always, unencouraging. Her husband is old and soon dies, so the chapter ends with her suddenly becoming a nun.

 ## 17 · E-AWASE

The Picture Competition/A Picture Contest
(3rd month of Genji's 31st year)

This chapter refers to the events of Chapter 14, "Miotsukushi." Rokujō's daughter, Akikonomu, is still desired by the now-retired Emperor Suzaku, but Genji has been working to have her made consort to the boy-emperor (his own son) out of respect for her late mother, whom he still thinks of fondly. Tō-no-Chūjō, however, is planning to have one of his daughters made consort to the boy-emperor. This boy is very fond of painting and this seems to put Akikonomu in a better position as she is an accomplished artist. Tō-no-Chūjō, not to be outdone, hires professional painters to regain the boy's interest in his daughter, Lady Chūjō of the new Kokiden apartments.

A picture competition ensues with Prince Hotaru (in W., Sochi), one of Genji's brothers, as judge. After some very interesting remarks about scrolls of earlier tales (scroll painting and tale writing/calligraphy were considered one art form), and as the competition gets heated, Genji introduces on Aki-konomu's side the scrolls he painted in exile, and wins the day. At the end of the chapter he is thinking of building a retreat to which he might soon retire.

松
風 *18 · MATSUKAZE*

The Wind in the Pine Trees/The Wind in the Pines
(Autumn of Genji's 31st year)

Genji is remodeling his palace at Nijō to accommodate various ladies, especially the Akashi lady and her child. The Akashi lady, however, is torn between a basic distrust of Genji and a desire to fulfill her father's hopes. Her father has some old property not far from the capital and decides to refurbish it for his daughter and wife (he must remain at Akashi) so they can be close to the court but away from the jealousies of Gen-ji's palace. As it happens, it is in Ōi (Katsura), right next to the retreat Genji has started to build and in the midst of some windswept pines (hence the title). After she is relocated there, Genji is eager to see her, but Murasaki demands most of his time. Finally, on the excuse of supervising details of his retreat, Genji steals away to Ōi. The lady is awed by Genji's courtly elegance, and he gets to see his daughter for the first time, now over two years old. He resolves to somehow bring her to court and put her under Murasaki's care. Other courtiers have followed Genji there and make it difficult for him to spend much time with the lady. Even the emperor hears he is there and sends messages.

Genji's entourage feasts there and must return to the capital without even a farewell to the Akashi lady. On his return, Murasaki is very jealous and makes life difficult, till Genji asks her if she might like to take charge of the small child. Her jealousy completely vanishes as her strong maternal instincts are at last released.

 19 · USUGUMO

A Wreath of Cloud/A Rack of Cloud
(Winter of Genji's 31st year to autumn of his 32nd year)

Genji presses his desire to have his daughter by the Akashi lady given over to him and Murasaki for proper aristocratic rearing. While the Akashi lady is heartbroken by the prospect, she is at last convinced, and Genji comes to remove the little girl to his palace at Nijō where Murasaki eagerly becomes a loving parent. About this time, Aoi's father, the prime minister, dies and Genji has to put off his own plans for retirement to take over the role of imperial advisor, for the country is beset by earthquakes and other foreboding signs. Then the worst blow of all falls with the death of Fujitsubo, aged thirty-seven. The title poem describes the sadness of the court at her passing.

A certain priest, who had been a confidant of Fujitsubo, comes to the young Emperor Reizei (in W., Ryōzen) and tells him that Genji is his real father. The emperor, feeling he has inadvertently violated precepts of filial piety by accepting rule while Genji, his true father, was never offered the title, sees this as the reason for the disasters and seeks to abdicate in favor of Genji; but Genji talks him out of it. Genji returns to his domestic affairs with Akikonomu, Murasaki, and the infant princess from Akashi. A subtle statement has been made about the importance of birth, which it is thought will discredit the infant, but which would not, after all, have been a barrier to Genji's accession.

朝
顔 *20 · ASAGAO*

The Morning Glory
(9th month of Genji's 32nd year to a snowy day that winter)

It is still the year of Fujitsubo's mourning and Genji, now thirty-two, is a more mature person; but he is still unable to forget a conquest. He has unsuccessfully pursued his cousin, Princess Asagao, for years. Now her father has died and she may quit her position as vestal at the Kamo Shrine. Genji visits her on the pretext of visiting their mutual aunt, but, to Genji's embarrassment, she is still unencouraging. He again encounters the elderly Lady of the Bedchamber (in S., Naishi) whose attentions are as unseemly as ever, and he meditates on old age and death. Murasaki worries that he has grown tired of her, but he returns to her in the end and they share recollections of various ladies, a scene that curiously resembles the rainy night conversation of Chapter 2. He has a disturbing dream in which Fujitsubo appears to him and chastises him for his role in her shame.

乙
女 *21 · OTOME*

The Maiden
(4th month of Genji's 33rd year to the 10th month of his 35th)

Yūgiri is now of age (his twelfth year) to enter the court. Genji decides not to lavish rank on him at this early point in his life; rather he bestows a low rank on him and enrolls him in the university to study the classics, much to Yūgiri's chagrin. Akikonomu is, after all, named empress to Reizei (in W., Ryōzen) and Tō-no-Chūjō is disappointed for his rejected daughter. Yūgiri is now gently courting a cousin, the second of Tō-no-Chūjō's daughters, who had been brought up with him. When Tō-no-Chūjō learns of this he grows angry and restricts his access to her. Yūgiri suffers from the policies of Genji and Tō-no-Chūjō, who well remember how wild they were at his age. Yūgiri's affair with this cousin (Lady Kumoi; in S., Kumoi-no-kari), is seen as roughly parallel to Genji's affair with his cousin, Asagao, but Yūgiri seems more successful. Kumoi's name is taken from the words, "wild goose in the clouds," of the poem she wrote indicating her longing to Yūgiri.

At court, Genji is selecting a Gosechi dancer and, after some competition in which, again, Tō-no-Chūjō is bested, Koremitsu's pretty daughter is chosen. Yūgiri sneaks a word with her and successfully starts his second amour. Here also we are reminded of an earlier and similar episode in Genji's life. But, as the year ends, Yūgiri is still feeling bad about his position as the "unpromoted marvel."

The following two years are hastily described in which Yūgiri finally gets his degree and is promoted, and Genji decides to get a larger estate, located in the area of Rokujō's old mansion. It is a magnificent palace, and all of Genji's women are at last able to share the same address. Akikonomu, in her autumn garden, exchanges poems with Murasaki, in her spring garden. And Genji is happy that there is harmony.

玉
鬘 *22 · TAMAKAZURA*

The Jeweled Chaplet
(End of Genji's 34th year—with flashbacks)

Genji is still supporting Ukon, the handmaiden of the late Lady Yūgao, but the whereabouts of Yūgao's daughter by Tō-no-Chūjō is not yet known to them. We learn that her nurse took the child with her when her husband assumed a post in faraway Kyūshū, totally ignorant of the fate of her mother. They ended up staying in Kyūshū much longer than they expected, and the poor child was raised to a young woman there.

By the time of the events of the last chapter, the young lady, now twenty, is being courted by an obnoxious yokel who has a great deal of power locally. To frustrate such attempts the nurse had circulated the deception that young Tamakazura, as she is called (in W., Tamakatsura), was deformed, but the lecherous yokel from Higo is persistent. Bribing and threatening everyone, he forces his suit upon her until the family of the nurse decides to set out quickly for the capital and hope for the best. After a hot pursuit, they seem to escape him and find themselves in Kyōto with no one to turn to and no place to stay. They decide to pray for aid at the famous Hatsuse Shrine where, miraculously, they meet Ukon. At last Genji hears of her and, with no complaint from Murasaki, brings her to his new mansion at Rokujō. She, as was Yūgiri, is placed under the care of "the lady of the orange blossoms" (in W., "the lady from the village of falling flowers"). As the chapter ends, Genji is very happy with the way things have turned out.

初
音 *23 · HATSUNE*

The First Song of the Year/The First Warbler
(New Year's of Genji's 36th year)

This chapter describes the New Year's celebrations of a very content Genji, now in his thirty-sixth year. He visits the various ladies at Rokujō and proceeds further to pay calls on Suetsumu Hana, "the safflower princess," and Utsusemi, "the lady of the locust shell," who is now, of course, a nun. In each case Genji is congratulating himself for his constancy and loyalty. At the end of the chapter, Tō-no-Chūjō's sons and Yūgiri come caroling, and Genji discerns that Yūgiri is not quite as good as Tō-no-Chūjō's son, Kōbai.

Incense pattern with butterfly design for Kochō.

胡
蝶 *24 · KOCHŌ*

The Butterflies
(3rd and 4th months of Genji's 36th year)

In the spring of this year, Genji has boats built to sail on his private lake and, of course, a party to celebrate the occasion. Murasaki decides this is a good time to answer Empress Akikonomu's poem about the superiority of seasons. Murasaki's spring garden is in its glory, and she has young attendants (in W., boys; in S., girls) dress up as birds and butterflies to present cherry blossoms and *yamabuki* (Japan globeflowers) to the empress with a poem which magnificently answers the empress' poem about autumn, found in Chapter 21, "Otome."

About this time, Tamakazura is being deluged by poems from possible suitors. Genji tries to advise her, but there are two major complications. First, everyone thinks she is Genji's daughter, so Yūgiri is put off because he thinks she is his sister, and Tō-no-Chūjō's sons (especially his eldest, Kashiwagi) are encouraged, being unaware that she is their sister. Prince Hotaru (in W., Sochi) and General Higekuro are the primary elder suitors, but the second complication is that Genji is himself falling in love with her. He attempts to reveal himself one evening (a scene reminiscent of the way he deflowered Murasaki) and is rejected, much to his chagrin. He reflects on the differences between parents and offspring.

螢 *25 · HOTARU*

The Glow Worm/Fireflies
(5th month of Genji's 36th year)

At Genji's insistence, Tamakazura finally receives his brother, Prince Hotaru (in W., Sochi). She is coy, though, and leaves much of their correspondence to her lady-in-waiting, Saishō. At one point, in the darkness, she even retires, unbeknown to Prince Hotaru. Genji has been watching all this and persuades her to return, after which he cleverly brings a bag of fireflies *(hotaru)* into her enclosure, and enough light is provided for Hotaru to catch a glimpse of her beauty. This is, of course, why he is referred to as Prince Hotaru (the firefly prince) in the Seidensticker translation.

After a day of equestrian archery contests for the younger set, Genji pays a friendly visit to "the lady of the orange blossoms," (in W., "the lady from the village of falling flowers") and stays the night, though in separate sleeping quarters.

The next day he stops by Tamakazura's apartments and finds her reading old romances. Genji at first chides her, but then confesses that he also reads them and that fiction is after all a legitimate art form.

The chapter ends with Tō-no-Chūjō wondering about the fate of his child by Yūgao. He has a dream which is interpreted as meaning that he has not taken proper care of unaccounted female offspring, and so he instructs his sons to watch for anyone claiming to be his daughter.

常
夏 *26 · TOKONATSU*

A Bed of Carnations/Wild Carnations
(Summer of Genji's 36th year)

On a hot summer day Genji is enjoying a picnic with some young friends of Yūgiri and begins to joke about Tō-no-Chūjō in front of Chūjō's son, Kōbai. Genji has heard of the search for long-lost daughters and heard rumors that one very countrified lady was found at Ōmi. Genji, by the way, is somewhat upset with Tō-no-Chūjō for frustrating Yūgiri's suit of Lady Kumoi.

Looking in on Tamakazura, he thinks about revealing her identity to Tō-no-Chūjō. Genji has not had much success with her and realizes any success he might have would only be damaging to her future. But as he sits with her and they begin to discuss the Japanese *koto,* she starts to soften to him. He begins to tutor her on the instrument, and his resolve to send her away is broken.

Meanwhile, Tō-no-Chūjō is trying to decide what to do about his new-found daughter, the lady from Ōmi. She is embarrassingly inelegant with a particularly loud and unsettling voice. He decides to send her to court with his other daughter, Lady Chūjō of the Kokiden apartments.

The carnations of the title are used to refer to Tamakazura and the lady from Ōmi as stray flowers picked out of their rustic circumstances.

篝火 *27 · KAGARIBI*

The Flares
(7th month of Genji's 36th year)

This is a short chapter in which Genji visits Tama-kazura for a romantic *koto* lesson. Leaving, he sees the watch flares are going out and writes a poem comparing his desire to a flare which would never go out. He goes off to a party of Yūgiri's friends who are playing the *koto* and flute. Tō-no-Chūjō's son, Kashi-wagi, is especially fine on the *koto* and Tamakazura overhears him pouring his heart into the music.

野分 *28 · NOWAKI*

The Typhoon
(8th month of Genji's 36th year)

It is autumn of the same year that has been chronicled since Chapter 23. Akikonomu is getting her garden in order to once again challenge Murasaki's, when a horrible storm strikes. The gardens are badly battered, and the storm has wreaked havoc. Yūgiri arrives to visit his father and accidentally catches his first glimpse of Murasaki. He is stunned by her beauty. In the general disarray, he is also able to observe Genji with Tamakazura, noting his more than parental affection for her. Later, he visits his grandmother who has been suffering from the disfavor of her son, Tō-no-Chūjō. Finally, Yūgiri visits his stepsister, the little princess from Akashi, and manages to write hasty letters to the ladies of his current affairs, Lady Kumoi and Koremitsu's daughter. The chapter ends with Tō-no-Chūjō complaining to his mother about the problems he has had with his daughters.

行
幸 *29 · MIYUKI*

The Royal Visit/The Royal Outing
(12th month of Genji's 36th year to the 2nd month of his 37th)

It is now the end of this notorious year, which might be called the year of Tamakazura, culminating in an imperial progress to Ōharano. It is, of course, a glorious affair, during which Tamakazura admires the beauty of the young emperor. Genji, who was unable to attend, had planned as much and later asks her if she might not be inclined to go to court in some capacity. Genji has decided he can no longer delay revealing her identity to Tō-no-Chūjō. It is time for her initiation ceremony, and her true parentage must be made known. This is unfortunately complicated by the ill-health of Chūjō's mother, Princess Ōmiya. Genji visits her to gauge her condition and to arrange a meeting with Tō-no-Chūjō. Chūjō is summoned and, at last, the news is broken to him. Genji and Chūjō strengthen their strained friendship, and the problem of Yūgiri and Kumoi is tactfully ignored.

After the initiation ceremony, they agree to recommend Tamakazura for the post of Lady of the Bedchamber (in S., "wardress"). At the end of the chapter, however, a comical scene occurs when the strange lady from Ōmi hears of all this and is indignant because she had her eye on the same post.

藤
袴 *30 · FUJIBAKAMA*

Blue Trousers/Purple Trousers
(8th and 9th months of Genji's 37th year)

Now that the secret of her parentage is generally known, Tamakazura is feeling very insecure about the change in all her relationships with people. Waley, for some reason, does not translate a major section of the chapter, including the scene in which she is visited by Yūgiri. Hoping to develop an affair with her, Yūgiri brings her the flowers, *fujibakama* (mistflowers), after which the chapter is named. He is not successful

Yūgiri pushing a spray of fujibakama flowers under the screen to the beautiful Tamakazura. This scene was copied from an early scroll painting.

and goes off to discuss, quite intelligently, her situation with his father, Genji. In fact, Yūgiri cleverly probes into Genji's feelings about her as well.

Waley takes up the story with Kashiwagi's visit to her. He has completely turned around from being the passionate suitor to become the sober brother delivering a message from their father. Distraught after Yūgiri's advances, she does not admit him to her presence anyway, so he is forced to communicate with her through her maid.

Tamakazura then sets about reviewing all the love letters and proposals she has received. It is incumbent upon her to select a husband soon, but she is not enthusiastic about any of the possibilities.

眞
木
柱 *31 · MAKIBASHIRA*

The Cypress Pillar
(10th month of Genji's 37th year to the 11th month of his 38th)

As this chapter starts, Tamakazura has already married, of all people, Higekuro. She is not happy about it, and seems to have consented out of a sense of fate rather than through any fondness for him. He has already been married, but this former wife, Murasaki's stepsister, is possessed with frequent fits of madness; her father, Prince Hyōbu (in W., Hyōbukyō), is angry with Higekuro and wants to take her and her children back to his home. In a final conversation with her, Higekuro seems to be reasoning with her when suddenly she pours a container of burning incense all over him, putting an end to any reconciliation.

Hyōbu has her brought back with their daughter. As they are leaving their home, the young daughter writes a poem about her favorite corner and its *makibashira* (of the title). When Higekuro learns of their departure he is upset, but loses little time installing Tamakazura in the vacated apartments. (Waley and Seidensticker disagree as to whom the name Makibashira should apply. Waley says Makibashira is Higekuro's mad wife; Seidensticker says Makibashira is Higekuro's beloved daughter.)

Meanwhile, the emperor is asking for Tamakazura,

who has taken the post of Lady of the Bedchamber (in S., "wardress"), to spend some time at court. Higekuro is finally persuaded to let her go, and she spends a happy day and night enjoying the splendor of the court and the presence of the emperor. Higekuro is impatient, openly, so she is given leave to go despite the emperor's desire that she remain. She goes home with Higekuro and settles down to bearing his children.

As the chapter ends, an amusing scene occurs when the strange lady from Ōmi makes a rather vulgar pass at Yūgiri.

梅
枝 *32 · UMEGAE*

The Spray of Plum Blossom/A Branch of Plum
(New Year's to the 3rd month of Genji's 39th year)

Genji begins elaborate preparations for his Akashi daughter's initiation ceremonies, hoping to impress the crown prince. The mixing of perfumes and incense is intricately described as it becomes a competition among all the members of Genji's household. Even Princess Asagao sends a surprise entry attached to a branch of plum *(umegae)*. Prince Hotaru (in W., Sochi) drops in and judges the various efforts. That evening the attention shifts to music, and Tō-no-Chūjō's son,

Kōbai (whose name means "rose plum"), sings the famous air "Umegae."

Untranslated by Waley is a final stage of the preparations in which Genji begins copying books and scrolls for his daughter's library. Finally, the ceremony is held and, with Empress Akikonomu officiating, it is magnificent.

Tō-no-Chūjō is, however, peeved at all this as it reminds him of his own daughters' lack of success at court. And now it seems that even the stand he took against Yūgiri has backfired since Yūgiri is now of distinguished rank and has received other proposals. Tō-no-Chūjō's and Kumoi's worries are groundless, as it turns out that Yūgiri still desires Kumoi.

藤
裏
葉　*33 · FUJI NO URABA*

Wisteria Leaves
(3rd to the 10th month of Genji's 39th year)

At a memorial service for his mother, the late Princess Ōmiya, Tō-no-Chūjō has the opportunity to approach Yūgiri and begin a reconciliation. He invites Yūgiri to a private wisteria-viewing party where they both relax and are able to dissolve their quarrel in wine and poetry. Feigning drunkenness, Yūgiri asks to stay the night and is helped by Kashiwagi to find Lady Kumoi's room. Their long-awaited union occurs at last.

Genji and Murasaki attend the Kamo River festival where he recalls the horrible ''carriage quarrel'' between Aoi and Rokujō. He now understands this to have been the fault of Aoi's arrogance, and he talks to Murasaki about the importance of benevolence. The conversation then turns to the sad condition of the Akashi girl's mother, of whom Murasaki had long been very jealous. They resolve to let her live now with her daughter at court.

Yūgiri and Kumoi refurbish and occupy the Sanjō mansion, and the chapter ends with a royal visit by the reigning emperor and Suzaku, the retired emperor, to Genji's palace at Rokujō.

若
菜
上 *34 · WAKANA: JŌ*

Young Shoots/New Herbs (Part One)
(12th month of Genji's 39th year to the 3rd month of his 41st)

Genji's stepbrother, the Retired Emperor Suzaku, has been ill and feels the time has come to renounce the world and become a Buddhist monk; but he has a favorite daughter, Nyōsan (in S., the Third Princess), who is yet dependent upon him. He had hoped to marry her to Yūgiri and is at a loss as to what to do with her now. He is advised not to marry her to anyone not of the blood royal, which rules out Kashiwagi and seems to leave Genji himself as the only acceptable candidate. Genji resists, but in the end is persuaded to take her to Rokujō.

Meanwhile, elaborate festivities are under way to celebrate Genji's fortieth birthday. The *wakana* (of the title) refers to the ritual herbs presented by Tamakazura. Shortly thereafter, Nyōsan is installed at Rokujō, and Murasaki is worried as never before, but she is careful not to display any signs of jealousy. Genji is, therefore, even more attracted to her for her magnanimity in adversity. Though Nyōsan is of higher birth than Murasaki, she is extremely immature and untutored. The whole affair makes Genji appreciate Murasaki more than before.

The little Akashi princess, who has been living with the crown prince, surprises everyone by becoming pregnant. She is released to Rokujō for delivery where she meets for the first time her now senile grandmother, the nun. And, by this accident, the princess learns that she was not born in the capital, so there is a terrible blot on her pedigree. Fortunately, this depressing information does not adversely affect her labor; she has a healthy boy, and returns to the palace of the crown prince a humbler person.

Now that things have settled down at Rokujō, Kashiwagi hopes to secretly start an affair with Nyōsan, who he thinks is being neglected by Genji anyway. Kashiwagi comes over to play a courtly version of football *(kemari)* with Yūgiri and some friends when, owing to the mischievousness of one of her cats, he and Yūgiri catch a fleeting glimpse of Nyōsan.

The chapter ends with Kashiwagi bent on contacting her, either through her maid, Kojijū, or even through her cat if necessary.

若
菜
下 *35 · WAKANA: GE*

Young Shoots/New Herbs (Part Two)
(3rd month of Genji's 41st year to the 12th month of his 47th)

About three years pass, during which time, though Waley fails to mention it, Makibashira (the daughter of Higekuro) is married off to Prince Hotaru (in W., Sochi). The emperor, who is Genji's son, abdicates and the eldest son of the Akashi princess is named crown prince.

Murasaki has been asking Genji's permission to become a nun, and he has been refusing it. A pilgrimage is conducted to thank the god of Sumiyoshi for his help during Genji's exile.

The Retired Emperor Suzaku enters his fiftieth year, and plans are made to celebrate it. This time the title refers to the herbs presented to Suzaku. Genji decides to give Nyōsan (in S., the Third Princess) extensive music lessons to prepare her for a special performance in Suzaku's honor, and Murasaki again shows her graciousness by refusing to become jealous. Genji contrasts her to Aoi and Rokujō and tells her how much more he loves her. Unfortunately, she suddenly falls ill. Genji's concern grows until all other activities come to a halt while he attends her.

Meanwhile, Kashiwagi is still trying to strike up an affair with Nyōsan. Now that Genji is thoroughly occupied, he has his chance. A nurse arranges a secret meeting at which he successfully seduces Nyōsan. Ominously, that night he dreams of a cat and, indeed, she turns out to have conceived.

Murasaki is near death when finally a medium lures the possessing spirit of Lady Rokujō out into the open. Her spirit is very angry over what Genji has said about her to Murasaki and begs him to have prayers dedicated to her soul's repose. Genji at once complies, and Murasaki gets better.

Hearing that Nyōsan is pregnant, Genji returns, but discovers a carelessly hidden letter from Kashiwagi revealing their tryst. Genji is disappointed and angry, but resolves to let the matter pass for Suzaku's sake. But when Kashiwagi learns of Genji's discovery, he becomes sick and ashamed ever to face Genji again.

(Facing page). The Retired Emperor Suzaku, now a Buddhist priest, administers vows to his daughter, Nyōsan, while her disappointed husband, Genji, looks on. This scene was copied from an early screen painting, preserving the high angular perspective (blown-away roof style).

柏
木 *36 · KASHIWAGI*

The Oak Tree
(New Year's to autumn of Genji's 48th year)

Kashiwagi is now desperately ill. His shame weighs heavily on him, and he doubts he will live much longer, so he writes to Nyōsan (in S., the Third Princess) one last time for some kind of resolution. They exchange emotional poems about their inevitable deaths. Nyōsan then goes into labor and delivers a son to be called Kaoru. He is a beautiful child, but painfully there is no resemblance to Genji, nor can Genji readily accept him. Nyōsan too is ill and begs permission to become a nun. Suzaku himself comes to visit and grants her

wish. Kashiwagi takes a turn for the worse and, in a last visit with Yūgiri, entreats his friend to intercede on his behalf with Genji and take care of his wife, Ochiba (in S., the Second Princess), after his passing. Kashiwagi then dies, never having seen his son. Yūgiri visits Ochiba and assures her of his protection. Poems are composed comparing the deceased to an oak tree, by which name he has already been referred to throughout the story.

横笛 *37 · YOKOBUE*

The Flute

(2nd month to autumn of Genji's 49th year)

Everyone is mourning Kashiwagi's passing. The Retired Emperor Suzaku is especially troubled, unable to obtain the proper religious detachment by his anxiety over the plight of his two daughters, Ochiba and Nyōsan (in S., the Second and Third Princess, respectively). Yūgiri continues to visit Ochiba and an attachment seems to be developing now that his ardor for Kumoi has had a chance to cool. On one such visit they play Kashiwagi's *koto,* and Ochiba gives him Kashiwagi's favorite flute. Back at home, Yūgiri feels smothered by Kumoi and his many children. In a disturbing sleep, he dreams of Kashiwagi who insists that the flute he was given is a personal heirloom.

Upset by this dream, the next day he seeks advice at Rokujō where he finds Genji playing with Kaoru and Prince Niou, the third son of the emperor and the Akashi princess. Genji unconvincingly lectures Yūgiri on propriety, but Yūgiri tries to get Genji to comment on his curious dream as well as on Kashiwagi's vague death-bed confession of an offense against Genji. Genji, however, remains evasive.

 38 · SUZUMUSHI

The Bell Cricket
(Summer to the 8th month of Genji's 50th year)

This chapter was not translated by Waley. It describes the fitting-out of a chapel for the newly ordained Nyōsan (in S., the Third Princess) at Rokujō. Yet, unsure how to deal with her, Genji continues to call on her and discomfit her about her affair with Kashiwagi; but Genji also pours himself into the preparations of her chapel, redecorating her garden in an autumn mode, complete with bell crickets, which provide the theme of the poems they compose to each other.

Later, he calls on Akikonomu whom he hopes to appoint as guardian for Kaoru so that Genji too can renounce the world. But she is also planning to enter the religious life to pray for her mother's soul which she now realizes is in torment.

夕
霧 *39 · YŪGIRI*

Evening Mist
(8th to 12th month of Genji's 50th year)

Ochiba (in S., the Second Princess) is still being consoled by Yūgiri when her mother falls ill and is moved to a villa in the north. Yūgiri attends them and decides that the time is ripe to make his desires known. Speaking with the lady that evening, he describes the evening mist, after which he is named. Then, unable to control himself, he pushes past her curtains and stops just short of having his way with her. She is shocked and dismayed and begs him to leave. Her mother is being attended by a chaplain who quickly relates the entire episode.

Meanwhile, Yūgiri has returned to his first wife, Kumoi, at Sanjō. When a letter comes from Ochiba's mother, Kumoi snatches it away in a fit of pique. Yūgiri pretends he has no interest in it and is unable to retrieve it till the next day. When no reply is forthcoming, Ochiba's mother assumes her daughter has been publicly jilted, has a relapse and dies.

Ochiba, feeling that Yūgiri is responsible, goes into a period of intense mourning for her mother. Yūgiri spends much time trying to console and care for her. On one occasion he attempts to force himself on her and she hides in a storeroom (closet). Meanwhile, his first wife, Kumoi, is so enraged by his neglect that she takes his daughters and goes home to her father, Tō-no-Chūjō.

Yūgiri goes home to Rokujō and complains to his nanny, "the lady of the orange blossoms" (in W., "the lady from the village of the falling flowers"), as he sadly compares his affairs to the good fortune Genji has had with the women of Rokujō.

He tries again to press his suit of Ochiba. This time, with the aid of her own maids and a back door to the storeroom, he is more successful and for the first time gets a proper look at her beauty. Still, however, he does not press his advantage, and they spend the night talking.

The chapter ends with Kumoi beginning to regret her hasty decision and a sympathetic exchange of poems between her and her old rival, Koremitsu's daughter (who has mothered five of Yūgiri's twelve children).

Yūgiri design.

Wisteria and water design.

御
法 *40 · MINORI*

The Law/The Rites
(3rd month to autumn of Genji's 51st year)

Back at Nijō, Murasaki begins formal preparations for her imminent death. A ritual offering of a thousand copies of the Lotus Sutra, that she had commissioned, is celebrated while the cherry blossoms are in spring bloom. Forced to face the unpleasant fact that she will precede him in death, Genji still cannot give her leave to take her final religious vows. Months pass and Murasaki languishes through the summer lovingly attended by the Akashi princess and the young Prince Niou. Then, in the autumn, as the princess is preparing to return to court, Murasaki suddenly dies, at almost the same time of year as Aoi had. Genji's grief is so extreme that Yūgiri, after stealing a last glimpse of the corpse, must take charge of the funeral arrangements.

幻 *41 · MABOROSHI*

Mirage/The Wizard
(New Year's of Genji's 52nd year to his death in the 12th month)

Genji enters seclusion at Nijō, interrupted briefly by his half brother, Hotaru (in W., Sochi), then by Prince Niou. Genji begins secretly planning to renounce the world and take holy orders. The Akashi lady advises him to wait, but his resolve grows and he determines to do so after his year of mourning for Murasaki. As Seidensticker's note informs us, the title refers to a famous Chinese poem in which an emperor sends a "wizard" off to find his dead consort in the nether world. This is the same reference that is made in the first chapter, and so a structural link is established.

Yūgiri manages the memorial services in his father's place and, as the year ends, Genji sadly disperses his property and destroys his old letters. Though it is not described, between this chapter and the next, Genji's death will have occurred. Some Japanese texts list an extra chapter, "Kumogakure" (The Light Behind the Clouds), existing only as a title to suggest a death sequence.

Tied love-note design.

匂
宮 *42 · NIOU MIYA*

Niou/His Perfumed Highness
(9 years after Genji's death—from the spring of Niou's 15th year to the New Year's of his 21st)

With Genji's passing, Yūgiri takes over Rokujō while the story shifts to the third generation. Niou and Kaoru, now young men, are the two most fascinating youths at court. Kaoru, ostensibly Genji's son, is now uneasy and curious about the events surrounding his mother's flight to the religious life. The Retired Emperor Reizei (in W., Ryōzen) and his empress, Akikonomu, who was childless, were entrusted with the care of Kaoru and see to his speedy promotion at court. Strangely, a subtle but pervasive fragrance unaccountably issues from his person,* and it is believed to be a special mark of virtue accumulated in a previous existence (see the section on *karma,* p. 40). Even though he does not actively pursue any relationships, he is very much sought after by all the ladies at court. Niou, on the other hand, is more headstrong and purposeful. He deliberately and artfully scents his robes to compete with Kaoru, and a friendly rivalry develops. (Niou's name means "perfumed highness," and Kaoru's name means "fragrant captain.")

   Emperor Reizei had one daughter by Lady Chūjō

---

* Plutarch records that a similar condition existed about the person of Alexander the Great.

(see Chapter 17, ''E-Awase''), and she is the subject of Niou's interest. Yūgiri's sixth daughter is also eligible and it is hoped that Kaoru will show interest.

紅梅 43 · *KŌBAI*

The Rose Plum
(Spring to winter of Niou's 25th and Kaoru's 24th year)

Replacing Tō-no-Chūjō as head of the Fujiwara clan is his eldest surviving son, Kōbai, who has married Makibashira (in W., the daughter of Makibashira),[1] the widow of Prince Hotaru (in W., Sochi). She already has a daughter from that union, and Kōbai has two daughters from his earlier marriage. With Makibashira, he at last fathers a son (in W., Tayū). Kōbai, operating as a typical Fujiwara, is intent upon marrying his daughters into the imperial family. He sends his eldest daughter (in W., Ōigimi) to the crown prince, even though Yūgiri's eldest daughter would already seem to be his favorite. He tries to interest Niou in the second daughter (in W., Naka-no-kimi). Using his page-boy son as a messenger with a branch of rose plum (hence the title and Kōbai's name), Kōbai does attract Niou's attention, but not to his second daughter so much as to the stepdaughter, who we see is extremely shy and retiring.

竹
河 *44 · TAKEKAWA*

Bamboo River

(Kaoru's 14th year to autumn of his 23rd)

This chapter takes up the story of Tamakazura (in W., Tamakatsura) related in Chapters 22–31. Her husband, Higekuro, has died and left her with some sons and two daughters, leaving specific instructions that the daughters should be married into the imperial family. In Seidensticker, the daughters are just referred to as "older" and "younger." Waley uses the Japanese titles "Himegimi" meaning "older daughter," and "Wakagimi" meaning "younger daughter."

Himegimi is very beautiful and attracts the suit of Yūgiri's and Kumoi's youngest son, whom Waley calls Kurōdo-no-Shōshō. He is insufferably ardent and, unfortunately, must compete with gallants like Kaoru who has also shown some interest in the girl. "Bamboo River" is the title of a song sung by Kurōdo and Kaoru as they attempt to court her. Kurōdo's feelings grow even stronger when he chances to observe the sisters playing a game of Go (in W., draughts) to win a favored cherry tree. It is the Retired Emperor Reizei (in W., Ryōzen), however, who finally wins her mother's approval. Apparently, Reizei still has an interest in Tamakazura herself, but he readily falls in love with Himegimi, who then bears him two children: a second daughter and his first son. This increases his favors to her so much that his two older ladies, Chūjō and Akikonomu, become very jealous.

Meanwhile, the present emperor is upset that he was not given first choice in the matter of Himegimi, so to placate him Tamakazura presents him with her second daughter, Wakagimi. But now people begin to think Tamakazura too presumptuous, pushing both daughters into the imperial family.

All her plans seem to have backfired. Higekuro's last wishes were as a curse, and Tamakazura is quite dejected as the chapter closes.

It should be remembered that the authorship of this chapter and the previous one is rather suspect. This chapter does not seem to relate very well to any of the following chapters, and the style is weaker and less polished.

橋
姫 *45 · HASHIHIME*

The Bridge Maiden/The Lady at the Bridge
(Kaoru's 20th year to the 10th month of his 24th year)

Sounding very much like the beginning of a new novel, this chapter starts by introducing a royal prince who turns out to be a younger stepbrother of Genji and who long ago was nearly maneuvered by Kokiden to be the crown prince over Genji's son, Reizei (in W.,

Ryōzen). Prince Hachi (in S., the Eighth Prince) is living in a kind of exile when, quite late in their lives, his wife gives birth to two daughters, then dies. Forced to live in a meager cottage at Uji, to the south of the capital, he becomes a kind of religious ascetic, even though his parental responsibilities keep him from becoming a priest.

Word of his saintliness reaches the court of Reizei where Kaoru is much impressed. He corresponds with the prince and they become fast friends studying Buddhist scriptures together. Once when Kaoru goes to visit, the prince is out, and so he meets the two daughters, Agemaki and Kozeri (in S., Ōigimi and Naka-no-kimi, respectively; not to be confused with Kōbai's daughters in W.). Agemaki, the elder, catches Kaoru's attention, as she represents the old dream of the hidden-away beauty who has fallen on hard times, first articulated in Chapter 2. Kaoru's poem to Agemaki, comparing her to the Uji Bridge maiden, demonstrates his overwhelming sympathy.

Back at court, though, he teases Niou with his account of the princesses, but the girls are both so shy and untutored that little comes of either the efforts of Niou or Kaoru. Fortunately, when Kaoru visits again, an elderly lady-in-waiting is there to coach the sisters, but when she sees Kaoru she almost forgets herself. It seems that she is Ben-no-kimi, daughter of the late Kashiwagi's nurse, who had been entrusted with the true story of Kaoru's birth. She, at last, tells him everything and gives him a parcel of Kashiwagi's old love letters to his mother.

椎
本 *46 · SHII GA MOTO*

At the Foot of the Oak Tree/Beneath the Oak
(2nd month of Kaoru's 23rd year to the summer of his 24th)

Niou makes a pilgrimage to a temple in the south, which allows him the opportunity to stop briefly at Uji on his return. Kaoru with him, he arranges to stay at a villa across the river from Prince Hachi's (in S., the Eighth Prince's) cottage. Of course, they are invited to cross the river and be entertained, but the Uji princesses are still not persuaded to present themselves.

Afterward, the prince begins to worry more and more about the fate of his daughters. He persuades Kaoru to accept some responsibility for them, but Kaoru is also planning to renounce the world to atone for his inauspicious birth and his consequent failure to have properly honored his true father, Kashiwagi. Kaoru's poem about the oak tree (of the title) expresses his regret at not having already become a monk like the prince. For his part, the prince now determines to leave the world entirely. He gives his daughters final instructions to beware of frivolous suitors and retreats to a nearby temple where, after a few days, he dies.

His daughters are truly crushed and mourn profusely, as does Kaoru, who had looked on the prince as the father he had never known. Niou also expresses regret, but his ulterior motives are apparent, and the Uji princesses are intimidated by his extreme elegance.

He tries to exchange poems with the younger daughter, Kozeri (in S., Naka-no-kimi), but only her sister, Agemaki (in S., Ōigimi), is up to the experience. Kaoru does his best to recommend Niou to them, without much success. As the chapter closes, it is summer and Kaoru manages to see through some screens how beautiful the two princesses are.

總
角 *47 · AGEMAKI*

Trefoil Knots
(8th to the 12th month of Kaoru's 24th year. Agemaki is 26; her sister, 24)

The title, "Agemaki," is a reference to a poem Kaoru writes to the elder of the Uji princesses comparing the tassels on the funeral altar to the braids of her hair, and it is used by Waley as her sobriquet, while Seidensticker calls her Ōigimi.

As the Uji princesses emerge from the prescribed period of mourning for their father, Kaoru and Niou follow up their respective suits. The elder sister, however, resists their advances as she thinks that her father's last wishes prohibited any kind of attachments at all. Kaoru is in an awkward position because, on the one hand, he had been unofficially appointed their guardian by Prince Hachi (in S., the Eighth

Prince), and on the other he has been serving as Niou's envoy to the younger sister. Furthermore, he himself is interested in Agemaki. Unfortunately, she feels the responsibility of her sister's care so much that she will only encourage Kaoru to marry Kozeri (in S., Naka-no-kimi), feeling that Niou is, as his reputation has it, a philanderer.

At last Kaoru carries out a desperate plan with the help of Ben-no-kimi, whereby he smuggles Niou into the younger sister's apartments and presses himself on Agemaki. Though, in conscience, Kaoru is unable to do more than restrain her for the evening, Niou completely compromises the more pliant Kozeri. With his mother, the empress, trying to convince him to marry Yūgiri's sixth daughter, Niou barely manages to come to Uji for each of the three nights that constitute a betrothal. On the third night he begs Kozeri to forgive him if he cannot always arrange to visit her, though, thanks to Kaoru's plan, they are now officially wed.

As was expected, on his return Niou is made a virtual prisoner at court for several months. Kozeri tries to understand, but Agemaki becomes completely distraught, assuming responsibility for the match, which she thinks now is not being treated seriously by Niou. Refusing to take food, Agemaki sickens and, in spite of Kaoru's most sincere efforts to sustain her, dies in a sequence reminiscent of Murasaki's death.

早
蕨 *48 · SAWARABI*

Fern Shoots/Early Ferns
(New Year's to the 2nd month of Kaoru's 25th year)

Mourning for her sister, Kozeri (in S., Naka-no-kimi) receives a poem and an offering of *sawarabi* from the abbot/teacher who had been her father's confessor. Meanwhile, Niou is planning to have her moved to the capital to live with him. Though she is worried about leaving her home to live without patronage at court, she is comforted and consoled by Kaoru who, she now realizes, was truly in love with her sister after all. Ben-no-kimi, too old to follow her to court, becomes a nun and remains at Uji.

As Kozeri is journeying to the capital, Yūgiri tries again to pressure Niou into marrying his daughter, Roku-no-kimi. Once Kozeri has arrived, though, it becomes obvious how strong his attachment is, and Yūgiri begins to consider Kaoru as an alternative candidate. Kaoru, however, flatly refuses. He would rather trail after Kozeri to be reminded of her beloved late sister.

Incense pattern for Sawarabi.

宿 木 *49 · YADORIGI*

The Mistletoe/The Ivy

(Summer of Kaoru's 24th year to the 4th month of his 26th year)

The emperor has a second daughter (by a now-deceased consort who had little influence at court) and he, comparing her to Kaoru's mother, Nyōsan or the Third Princess (see Chapter 34), has in mind to marry her to Kaoru, even though Kaoru is not a prince of the blood. Of course, Kaoru's mind is still on Agemaki (in S., Ōigimi), so the emperor's hints in this area are at first lost on him.

Similarly, Niou is under increasing pressure to marry Yūgiri's daughter, Roku-no-kimi, and a marriage is soon arranged just as his prior wife, Kozeri (in S., Naka-no-kimi), has become pregnant. Kaoru begins to visit her to console her and to share their grief for her sister. Slowly, though, his heart opens to her, and he finds himself wishing he had taken her for himself as Agemaki had once suggested.

Niou discovers Kaoru's distinctive scent in his wife's robes when he returns and, suspecting the worst, he burns with jealousy. Kozeri does not want to suffer any more of his suspicion, so when Kaoru returns she tells him of an illegitimate half sister of hers who much resembles Agemaki. Her attempt to put him off succeeds: he is immediately curious and decides to seek out Ben-no-kimi for more information.

Yadorigi design.

Here Waley breaks the chapter in two, continuing with the second half in part six of his serialization.

At Uji, Kaoru quizzes Ben-no-kimi for more information about Ukifune (as Waley has already begun to refer to her). They write poems about a sprig of *yadorigi* (mistletoe) which Kaoru plans to bring back to Kozeri as a momento of her sister. Before leaving, he makes arrangements to have the Uji villa converted into a temple. Back in Kyōto he is promoted in rank as Kozeri safely gives birth to a son, thus strengthening her position with Niou.

Kaoru himself finally submits to the emperor's wishes and marries the Second Princess (not Ochiba; see Appendix 1, p. 170). A wisteria banquet is described, and everyone expresses the opinion that Kaoru has been fortunate to marry above his station. But, as the chapter ends, Kaoru is back at Uji where he chances to arrive on the same day that Ukifune has come to pay homage to her late father's memory. He finds a peep hole and catches a furtive glimpse of her beauty.

東
屋 *50 · AZUMAYA*

The Eastern House/The Eastern Cottage
(8th and 9th months of Kaoru's 26th year. Ukifune is 21.)

In Hitachi, Ukifune is being carefully watched over by her mother, while her unlettered stepfather is more concerned about his own daughters' futures. A certain guards lieutenant (in W., Sakon) attempts to ally himself to this powerful governor by proposing marriage to Ukifune. At the last minute, though, he is told that she is only an adopted daughter, so he has his go-between rearrange the marriage between him and the governor's favorite daughter (in S., Himegimi). Humiliated by this cruel turn of events, Ukifune is taken away by her mother and graciously accepted at the house of her royal half sister, Kozeri (in S., Naka-no-kimi).

Unfortunately, Niou catches Ukifune alone one evening and, but for a timely imperial summons, would have had his way with her. Ukifune's mother and Kozeri are told of this and, to Kozeri's great embarrassment, the mother takes Ukifune off to an unfinished cottage (of the title), where it is hoped she can remain secure.

Meanwhile, Kaoru has at last overcome his own scrupulous sense of modesty enough to begin inquiries after her. Contacting Ben-no-kimi at Uji, he persuades her to conduct him to Ukifune's retreat, where their fated union at last takes place. Then he steals her off

to his own villa at Uji and lovingly commences her
social training with *koto* lessons, reminiscent of the
way Genji set out to instruct Murasaki at the end of
Chapter 5.

浮
舟 *51 · UKIFUNE*

A Boat upon the Waters
(New Year's to the 3rd month of Kaoru's 27th year)

From Uji, Ukifune sends New Year's gifts to Kozeri (in
S., Naka-no-kimi) and her young son. This rouses
Niou's interests. Remembering how Kaoru often
has visited Uji in the past months, he decides to commence an investigation. Enlisting the aid of a son-in-
law of one of Kaoru's retainers, Niou learns all about
Ukifune and, in secret, rushes out there for himself.
Cleverly, he exploits the darkness, is mistaken for
Kaoru, and let into her chambers. Before she realizes
it, Ukifune is once again in Niou's clutches, and so
she remains till the next day. Though she and her
mother were planning a pilgrimage to Ishiyama, Niou
refuses to leave her, and once again he has his way.
When he finally does leave, he is so lovesick at court
people worry for his health. Not knowing the true
cause of Niou's malady, even Kaoru pays him a visit,
but Niou is hardly comforted.

Meanwhile, Ukifune is receiving letters almost daily from both Kaoru and Niou, each promising his love and asking her to move into a special hideaway with him. Niou boldly visits her again and takes her off in a boat across the wild river to a farmhouse. On board they exchange poems, she describing herself as a boat upon the waters (her name and the chapter title) as she starts to fall in love with him. Now loving both, she cannot bear the thought of refusing either and slowly realizes her only solution is to drown herself in the river.

As more and more letters are sent to Uji, the two messengers begin to notice each other. Kaoru's man has the other followed, and Niou's secret is uncovered. Unsure of what to do, Kaoru scolds the guards he has stationed at Uji, and they begin to tighten their security. When Niou comes out again, he is unable to get through and must talk only with Jijū, a sympathetic maid.

Ukifune's situation is desperate. Her maid expects her to be Niou's mistress, and her mother expects her to be Kaoru's. Totally forlorn, her only recourse now is to compose herself for the inevitable and throw herself into the wild current of the Uji River. She burns her letters and turns her thoughts to death.

Incense pattern for Ukifune.

蜻
蛉 *52 · KAGERŌ*

The Gossamer Fly/The Drake Fly
(3rd month to autumn of Kaoru's 27th year)

Ukifune has disappeared, and Ukon, Jijū, and the rest at Uji are frantic as slowly they conclude that she must have thrown herself into the river. Niou's messenger arrives and is told Ukifune has died, supposedly of natural causes (suicide was considered sinful), and a mock funeral pyre is hastily cremated. Back in the capital, Niou throws himself into profuse and agonized mourning. Kaoru, better able to cope with his grief, visits Niou to gauge the depth of Niou's feelings for her. In a scene curiously reminiscent of the visit he paid Niou in the previous chapter, Kaoru, himself cold and at least outwardly dispassionate, is like an emotional voyeur. Hungry for more details of the sad event, Niou sends Tokikata who brings Jijū back to the capital for interrogation, while Kaoru goes to Uji himself to question Ukon. Thus they are both told that Ukifune had committed suicide over the impossible position their caprices had created for her.

Niou's grief is dramatic but untroubled by remorse; unlike Kaoru's which makes him write to Ukifune's mother and offer to provide backing for her other children. Niou, on the other hand, attempts to mollify his grief by pursuing new romantic conquests. Kosaishō, a beautiful attendant to Niou's sister, the First Princess, attracts his fancy, but she, aware of his reputation for philandering, shuns him in favor of Kaoru. Kaoru, however, is more interested in the First Princess herself, an old playmate of his whom he is able to secretly observe applying an icicle to her bare neck and shoulders in the sweltering heat. He cannot help but contrast her to his wife, the rather plain Second Princess.

Meanwhile, another lady arouses his concern. Miya-no-kimi, the young daughter of the now-deceased Prince Shikibu, is without support at court and is forced to accept a post with the empress as an attendant. Her condition reminds Kaoru painfully of Uki-fune and Agemaki (in S., Ōigimi), so he offers her his heart-felt consolation and sympathy.

As the chapter ends, Kaoru writes a poem to a *kagerō* (of the title), which comes to represent the illusory and fleeting rewards of love in his life.

手
習 *53 · TENARAI*

Writing Practice/At Writing Practice
(3rd month of Kaoru's 27th year to the 4th month of his 28th year)

There is an elderly Bishop (Sōzu) of Yokawa on Mt. Hiei whose aging mother, a nun, is taken ill on a pilgrimage to Hatsuse, so it is necessary to stop at Uji. Here, in the grounds of the abandoned mansion of

Suzaku, they discover the sickened body of Ukifune. The younger sister (in W., Imōto) of this bishop had also become a nun upon the untimely death of her daughter, and when she sees Ukifune, she transfers her motherly affection and, taking her to their retreat at Ono, endeavors to nurse Ukifune back to health.

At first, Ukifune is on the point of death and can remember nothing, but the bishop comes and, with the aid of Kannon, exorcises the malign spirit of an ex-cleric from her, after which she begins to recover. Thereafter, the dead daughter's widower (in W., "the colonel"; in S., "the captain") stops by and catches a glimpse of Ukifune's long hair, which excites him to write many poems in suit to her. Ukifune, however, has learned her lesson and flatly refuses to answer any of his poems, forcing Imōto to write replies for her.

As her memory returns, she grows even more reclusive. Now repenting her affair with Niou and realizing the greater worth of Kaoru, she has only her writing practice to confide in and console herself with. She finally makes up her mind to renounce the world and become a nun herself. Imōto is opposed to this kind of drastic step in one so young and beautiful, so Ukifune takes advantage of an occasion when Imōto is on a pilgrimage and the bishop is stopping on his way to minister to the sickened First Princess. The bishop administers her vows, cuts her hair, and she becomes a nun.

At court, the bishop effects a miraculous cure of the First Princess, and later, chatting with the empress, tells her the whole story of his discovery of Ukifune. Realizing that this is probably the very woman in whom Kaoru and her son had been so interested, the empress has her woman, Kosaishō, tell Kaoru of the bishop's story. Kaoru then resolves to go to Yokawa for confirmation.

54 · *YUME NO UKIHASHI*

The Bridge of Dreams/The Floating Bridge of Dreams
(Summer of Kaoru's 28th year)

Kaoru visits the bishop (Sōzu) at Yokawa and tries to act unconcerned as he asks about Ukifune. The bishop, feeling now some regret for what he has done, carefully relates the incidents of her discovery and exorcism, hoping that Kaoru will, at least, understand his actions. Kaoru tries to pass it off, but it is evident he is much disturbed, and he asks the bishop to take him immediately to see her. Thinking that unwise, the bishop is, however, persuaded to write her a note to be delivered by Kaoru's page, her stepbrother from Hitachi.

At Ono, Ukifune, hearing the familiar approach of Kaoru's outriders, retreats further into her prayers. The other nuns have a difficult time making her read the bishop's letter. And though she is moved to tears, she firmly resolves not to admit her identity to anyone. Not even her stepbrother, with a second letter of appeal from Kaoru, can change her mind.

The Tale ends with Kaoru wondering if there is not some other lover involved.

PART THREE

For Further Study

VIII

Notes on the Structure of the Novel

Murasaki Shikibu most certainly did not write this novel in a single effort for publication. Her audience was the tight-knit society of the Heian court, and her manuscripts, in the form of handwritten notebooks, were passed around, read, and sometimes copied simultaneously. If one were extremely fortunate, a whole set of these chapters, still individually bound, might eventually be acquired. There are, sadly, no surviving manuscripts in her own hand. While she was writing, though, it seems likely that people were reading them voraciously, yet only by chance in the chronological sequence in which they are arranged today. In every chapter Lady Murasaki carefully and subtly provides references to the general chronology of the events, covering in all exactly seventy-five years from the birth of Genji to the events of the last chapter. But the chapters were not originally numbered, nor do we have any evidence indicating the order in which the chapters were actually composed.

Readers of the Waley translation are, no doubt, sorely tempted to regard the subtitle, "A Novel in Six Parts," as indicative of the intended structure of the novel. Strangely, Waley himself seemed to have submitted to that allure, for, in his introduction to *The Bridge of Dreams,*[1] he treats his six parts as established structural divisions when, in fact, the novel was never so construed. Any analysis of the structure of *The Tale of Genji* must first admit that the only divisions clearly expressed by the author in composition are the fifty-four *jō,* which have come to be referred to as chapters or quires and which vary considerably in length from only a page or two to the voluminous "Wakana" chapters, 34 and 35.

The whole task of structural analysis, therefore, tends in a most sinister way to assume a Western orientation, of which Lady Murasaki could not possibly have been aware. Yet, if we are willing to acknowledge the pitfalls and purely speculative nature of any conclusions that might be drawn, such an analysis might teach us something about *The Tale of Genji* after all.

Despite the serialized nature of its composition, *The Tale of Genji* has an organic structure that cannot be neatly severed into discrete plot segments other than the originally designed chapters. A story may begin in one chapter, recede for several more, then break out in a chapter further on, while other subplots are developing at their own, very practical rate with similarly measured thrusts. Plots overlap and tangle in a complicated and totally realistic fashion.

Only once is there a clear break in the flow of all

the plots: after Chapter 41, "Maboroshi," with the death of Genji. The following chapter, "Niou," jumps ahead nine years and resembles closely a back-by-popular-demand sequel. Yet, usually, of the last thirteen chapters, only the last ten, beginning with "Hashihime," are thought of as a unit. The so-called "Uji-jūjō," or the Ten Quires of Uji, is sometimes regarded as a separate work.

At any rate, beyond this one break after the death of Genji, on which all of the studies of the novel agree, there is little concurrence, though most will agree that there is a basic outline of Genji's rise in the world, followed by his decline. One very definite aspect of the novel's construction that tends to support a two-part formula is what Waley described as "balancing" scenes. Throughout the latter parts of the novel there are curious echoes or parallel scenes, the most famous being Genji's discovery that the wife he took in his latter years has cuckolded him in the same way that he deceived his father by seducing Fujitsubo.

Though few scholars consider it a structural division, for the sake of convenience another set of ten has often been distinguished: the Ten Quires of Tamakazura (Chapters 22–31), whose story is enough of a separate intrigue to warrant such special attention. But we cannot ignore the fact that, even within these chapters, links with other subplots continue from the earlier sections while new sequences begin only to find resolution much later.

It is tempting, further, to look for other groups of

ten, which, with some exception, would mathematically compute very easily. Many scholars and stylists, for instance, believe that "Kōbai," Chapter 43, and "Takekawa," Chapter 44, were not written by Lady Murasaki and were probably written sometime after her death, then included, or rather inserted, in their chronological place in the novel. Furthermore, Chapter 1, "Kiritsubo," is believed to have been composed by Lady Murasaki well after the other chapters, to serve as an introduction for a work that had by then become very popular. "Niou Miya," Chapter 42, seems very similar to "Kiritsubo" in construction and function and, therefore, may also have been composed apart as an introduction for insertion.

If all this supposition is correct (and it is a considerable amount of supposition at that), one possible view of the structure might look like this:

Part 1: The Ten Quires of Genji's Youth
(Chapters 2–11) before which Chapter 1, "Kiritsubo," was later added as an introduction.

Part 2: The Ten Quires of Genji's Rise
(Chapters 12–21)

Part 3: The Ten Quires of Tamakazura
(Chapters 22–31)

Part 4: The Ten Quires of Genji's Demise
(Chapters 32–41)

Part 5: (The Sequel). The Ten Quires of Uji
(Chapters 45–54) before which Chapter 42, "Niou," was later added as an introduction.

The major flaw in this plan is that it supposes the Ten Quires of Uji to be complete in the author's design, and this supposition is a point still being debated by scholars. Even the last chapter, "Yume no Ukihashi" (The Bridge of Dreams), does seem to end in the middle of things, as if Lady Murasaki just abruptly stopped writing one day. Interestingly enough, the two major English translators are divided on this very issue.

Waley argues that the last chapter "ends with a combination of particles used exclusively to mark the close of a chapter," and that the very title "The Bridge of Dreams leads nowhere, breaks off like the tattered edge of a cloud."[2] But could not these particles have been added by a well-meaning editor to clean things up for circulation? And even if that chapter was meant to end the way it does, the possibility of additional, intended chapters, never finished or maybe lost, is not ruled out. On the other hand, Seidensticker feels:

> . . . that it stands at the beginning rather than at the end of something. An altogether drier, more laconic story should follow; and that it does not is, once again, a strong argument for the theory of single authorship. Only Murasaki herself had come far enough to be up to it, and when she faltered, there was, as with Genji, no one to take her place.[3]

As was pointed out above, Lady Murasaki was following no model, domestic or foreign. She invented her structure as she went along, drawing on her experience in the Heian court, and following the innate drift of the literature of her day. In the process, she helped shape the very essence of her country's literary aesthetics. It is left to us only to hypothesize and, if we are able, to learn something of her genius from the effort.

IX

Critical Questions for Study

The *Genji Monogatari* did not simply arise out of airy nothingness. The word *monogatari* 物語 (lit., "thing spoken," and generally translated as "tale") represented a literary or folkloric genre from which Murasaki Shikibu was able to draw, as can plainly be seen from the many references in the story to "romances of old." But, clearly, Murasaki, through what must have been a deliberate concentration on the psychological depth and dimension of her characters, wrought out of those whimsical fantasies of the past her country's, and quite possibly the world's, first real novel.

Twice the length of *War and Peace,* it is more often compared with modern European works like Proust's *À la Recherche du temps perdu* than with products of its own Heian period. Indeed, it has itself been the subject of several thousand volumes of criticism and appraisal, and the greatest of Japanese poets, novelists, and dramatists through the centuries have paid homage to its influence. Some of the most famous Noh, Kabuki, and Bunraku dramas are actually based on its plots, and *haiku* and *waka* poems too many to number draw strength from allusions to it.

To guide the student who would delve more deeply into a critical appreciation of the greatness of this work, I suggest here some questions to stimulate a closer reading.

1. In what way does the author relate the poetic sobriquets she has assigned to her various characters to their personalities or their functions in the plot, the theme, or the mood of the novel?

2. From evidence in the text, what kind of portrait can we assemble of what Genji would consider to be the perfect woman? Does this ideal change in any way as the novel progresses?

3. Looking carefully at the rainy night conversation in Chapter 2, connect as many of the ladies that are later encountered as possible. Is there any observable pattern, or theme?

4. Of all Genji's affairs, which have had the most impact on him? What sort of impact was it, and what significance can we assume it to have to the theme or themes of the whole novel?

5. What is the purpose or possible function to the novel of the relationship between Genji and Tō-no-Chūjō? What might be the significance of their alienation in the latter books? Is Tō-no-Chūjō a foil to Genji? If so, does he cease to be a foil as their friendship wanes?

6. Find as many passages as you can that comment directly on Genji's character. Can we accept these at face value, or does Genji seem to be misunderstood even by the narrator?

7. Study carefully the important female characters: Yūgao, Fujitsubo, Murasaki, Tamakazura, and Ukifune. Is there any thematic pattern that can be discerned?

8. Kokiden, Aoi, Rokujō, and the Third Princess of Emperor Suzaku (called Nyōsan by Waley) are all women out of Genji's favor. Do they share any common fault(s) that might explain his disfavor, or does this just indicate Genji's capriciousness?

9. Compare and contrast the principal male characters: Genji, Yūgiri, Kashiwagi, Niou, and Kaoru. What pattern is discernible?

10. Why is Genji's son, Yūgiri, so undistinguished? Tō-no-Chūjō's son, Kashiwagi, seems to be much more like Genji than Yūgiri. What significance could the author have had in mind for this break in the blood-line? (Read over the essay on religions, especially the material on *karma,* p. 40.)

11. Of the three major characters in the Uji Quires (Niou, Kaoru, and Ukifune), on which would you say the author was trying to focus our attention and interest, and what thematic significance might that have?

12. How does the author use place and time to create appropriate moods or psychological atmosphere for the various events of the novel? Does she use

it more effectively in the early sections or the later chapters?

13. It has been observed that there are many parallel scenes in the novel. Point out as many as you can, and compare them carefully for similarities and differences.

14. How effectively does the poetry work in the novel? Take a sample scene or chapter and show how the poems are being used.

15. To which modern authors can Murasaki Shikibu be compared? In a short paper, illustrate and defend your answer, relating your remarks to Genji's comments on the nature and use of fiction that appear in Chapter 25, ''Hotaru.''

Appendixes

1. Names, Titles, and Sobriquets, Cross-indexed for the Waley and Seidensticker Translations

Anyone attempting to compare translations of the *Genji Monogatari* will very likely find confusing the different ways by which characters, even main characters, are identified in different texts. These divergences are the result of the fact that it was considered discourteous to refer to members of the Heian aristocracy by their actual names. Yet one of the marvels of the novel's construction is the complex cast of characters of which Murasaki Shikibu never loses track, no matter how loose the plot line seems to be.

In the original, Murasaki uses several means to identify characters. First, she will occasionally, for the more memorable characters, assign a poetic epithet or sobriquet which is usually attached to a character through a poem written by, to, or about her or him. Yūgao, for instance, is named after the flower "evening faces" by Genji because of the incidents surrounding his discovery of her in Chapter 4. There is evidence, though, that Tō-no-Chūjō, who had known her previously, associated her with the flower *tokonatsu* (carnation or bedflower).

Secondly, a character may also be known by the name of the place where she lives. Genji's first wife, Lady Aoi (heartvine), is also sometimes referred to as "the lady at Sanjō" (the third ward). And the infamous Lady Rokujō's name means literally, "the lady of the sixth ward."

Finally, courtiers were known primarily by their ranks in the rather complex Confucian bureaucracy adapted from

China. Genji's friend and rival, Tō-no-Chūjō, therefore, was actually a member of the Fujiwara family, but his name, as it appears in both English translations, identifies him as a particular sort of captain, a rank which he possesses only in the first few chapters. In the original, he is subsequently known by such ranks as Councillor, Privy Secretary, and Minister of the Left. Women who did not hold these ranks might still be referred to by the name of the rank assigned to their husbands as, for example, the author herself is called Shikibu because of her family's connection with the Bureau of Rites. To simplify matters somewhat for the modern reader, Waley and Seidensticker have frequently selected Japanese terms of ranks and permanently assigned them to certain characters.

I have here provided an alphabetical listing of characters, cross-referenced for both translations, and included numbered designations under any name or title that refers to more than one character.

*   *   *

AGEMAKI 總角 (lit., trefoil knot or tassel). Title of Chapter 47. In Waley, she is the eldest daughter of Prince Hachi and, consequently, one of the Uji princesses. In Seidensticker, she is called Ōigimi.

AKASHI LADY 明石上 Akashi-no-ue (lit., lady from the province of Akashi). The daughter of a former governor of Akashi; she is met and wooed by Genji during his exile.

AKASHI PRINCESS 明石御方 Akashi mikata (lit., Akashi highness). She is the daughter of Genji and the Akashi lady. She was born inauspiciously in the province, and yet at the end of the novel she is the empress (Chūgū) to Kinjō, son of the Emperor Suzaku.

AKIKONOMU 秋好 (lit., lady who loves autumn). The daughter of Lady Rokujō, she is made vestal at Ise Shrine. Later she is consort, then empress (Chūgū), to Reizei. In some Japanese sources she is called Umetsubo.

AMIDA BUDDHA 阿彌陀佛 Amida Butsu (in Sanskrit, *Amitabha*). A manifestation of Buddha through whose intercession one may reach the Bliss of the Western Paradise.

AOI, LADY 葵の上 Aoi-no-ue (lit., lady of the heartvine/ hollyhock). Title of Chapter 9. Genji's first wife, a Fujiwara; Tō-no-Chūjō's sister. She dies of demonic possession, attributed to the jealousy of Lady Rokujō.

ASAGAO 朝顔 (lit., morning face; the flower, morning glory). Title of Chapter 20. Daughter of Genji's uncle, Prince Momozono, and the object of Genji's unrequited affection.

ATEKI あてき (phonetic value only). (1) An orphaned girl in the service of Lady Aoi. Genji takes her in after Aoi dies. In Waley, she is called Miss Ateki. (2) The daughter of Shōni and Tamakazura's nurse.

AZECHI-NO-KIMI 按察君 (lit., Miss Azechi). A young maid of Kaoru's mother, favored by Kaoru.

BEN-NO-KIMI 辯君 (lit., Miss Ben). The daughter of Kashiwagi's nurse; later a maid to the Uji princesses, she eventually becomes a nun (辯尼 Ben-ama).

BEN-NO-OMOTO 辯御許 (lit., Ben of the imperial apartments). (1) In Seidensticker, the maid of Tamakazura who encouraged Higekuro's suit of her mistress. (2) A precocious and impudent lady-in-waiting to the Akashi empress with whom Kaoru exchanges frivolities; said by Waley to be a take-off of the author's famous contemporary, Sei Shōnagon.

BUGO-NO-SUKE 豊後介 Bugo/Bungo-no-suke (lit., vice-governor of Bugo; a province in Kyūshū). In Waley, the son of Shōni and Tamakazura's nurse.

CHAMBERLAIN. See Jijū (2).

CHŪGŪ 中宮 (lit., middle palace). The title of empress as bestowed by an emperor on his most favored consort. See Emperors and Empresses.

CHŪJŌ 中将 (lit., middle commander; a rank equivalent to captain). (1) A nickname for Genji's old friend and rival, Tō-no-Chūjō. (2) Genji's rank in the very early chapters. (3) A woman in attendance upon Utsusemi.

CHŪJŌ, LADY 中将君 Chūjō-no-kimi (lit., miss of the captaincy). Sometimes referred to as Lady Chūjō of the new Kokiden apartments. The eldest daughter of Tō-no-Chūjō, she is an imperial consort who competes unsuccessfully with Akikonomu for favor with the Reizei emperor; she bears the emperor one daughter, Ichi-no-miya.

CHŪNAGON 中納言 (lit. middle councillor). A fairly common name for various women in attendance upon such ladies as Aoi, Oborozukiyo, and others. One of Aoi's ladies of whom Genji is especially fond.

COLONEL, THE 中将 Chūjō (lit., middle commander). In Waley, he is a widower of the daughter of the nun of Ono; he tries unsuccessfully to court Ukifune at

Ono. In Seidensticker's translation, he is called "the captain."

DAINI-NO-NAISHI 大貳內侍 (lit., second principal palace attendant). An art connoisseur among the ladies in the court of the young Emperor Reizei. She takes Chūjō's daughter's side in the picture competition.

EIGHTH PRINCE. See Hachi, Prince.

EMPERORS and EMPRESSES. The novel compasses the reigns* of four emperors:

1. Emperor Kiritsubo 桐壺帝 (lit., pawlonia apartments emperor). Usually called "the old emperor," he is the father of Genji. Fujitsubo becomes his empress; his reign runs through to the end of Chapter 8.

2. Emperor Suzaku 朱雀帝 (lit., red sparrow emperor). Son of Emperor Kiritsubo and Lady Kokiden; Genji's stepbrother; his empress is Oborozukiyo; his reign runs through Chapter 14.

3. Emperor Reizei 冷泉帝 (lit., cool fountain emperor). Called Ryōzen by Waley, he is supposedly the old emperor's son, but in reality he is Genji's son by Empress Fujitsubo; Reizei's reign runs through Chapter 35.

4. Emperor Kinjō 今上 (lit., present majesty). Simply referred to as emperor regnant in the final

---

* *Note:* An emperor's reign more often ends with his abdication instead of his death. In each case above, the emperor continues to function as a character after his abdication and is known as the **retired emperor.**

chapters, he is Suzaku's son and his empress is Genji's daughter, the Akashi princess.

EVENING FACES. See Yūgao.

FALLING FLOWERS, LADY FROM THE VILLAGE OF. See Hanachiru Sato.

FIFTH PRINCESS. See Nyōgo.

FIRST PRINCESS 女一宮 Onna Ichi-no-miya (lit., first princess). (1) The daughter of Lady Chūjō and the Reizei emperor. (2) The first-born daughter of the Akashi empress and the emperor regnant in the last chapters; she is the elder sister of Niou and the beloved of Kaoru.

FUJITSUBO 藤壺 (lit., wisteria apartments; see p. 179). The favored consort of Genji's father after the death of Kiritsubo, whom she resembles. Genji falls in love with her; she is the mother of Reizei and she becomes empress (Chūgū) to Genji's father.

GENJI, PRINCE HIKARU 光源氏 Hikaru Genji (lit., shining prince of the Minamoto clan). Son of the old emperor and his beautiful but tragically maligned consort, Kiritsubo. He is the romantic hero of this novel whose surpassing beauty and talents seem to belong to a bygone era, but are the epitome of Heian aesthetics.

GOSECHI DANCER 五節君 Gosechi-no-kimi (lit., miss of the group of five). A ceremonial dancer; one of five maidens selected from the lower ranks of the aristocracy, but not beneath the romantic interests of Genji **and**, later, Yūgiri.

HACHI, PRINCE 八宮 Hachi-no-miya (lit., eighth prince). A younger brother of Genji who was exploited by Kokiden, then exiled when Genji came to power. Living at Uji as a sainted layman, he fathers two daughters known as the Uji princesses. In Seidensticker, he is known as the Eighth Prince.

HANACHIRU SATO 花散里 (lit., village of falling flowers). Title of Chapter 11. The younger sister of Reikeiden, a consort of Genji's father. After his death, Genji takes charge of her, though she is no great beauty, and she later becomes a sort of nanny to Yūgiri, then, Tamakazura. In Waley, she is known as "lady from the village of falling flowers"; in Seidensticker, "lady of the orange blossoms."

HEI NAISHI 平内侍 (lit., palace attendant of the Hei quarters). An art connoisseur among the ladies of young Emperor Reizei's court; she takes Akikonomu's side in the picture contest.

HIDARI UMA-NO-KAMI 左馬頭 (lit., left captain of the horse). One of the young gallants who shares his experiences with Genji in the rainy night conversation of Chapter 2. In Seidensticker, he is called simply "a guards officer."

HIGEKURO 髭黒 (lit., black beard). The uncle of Emperor Kinjō and the brother of Lady Jōkyōden; husband of Murasaki's mad sister; later he marries Tamakazura. According to Seidensticker's note (p. 424 of his translation), he is the most important statesman in the land after Genji and Tō-no-Chūjō.

HIGO, THE BUMPKIN OF 大夫監 Taifu-no-gen (lit., from the first rank inspector's office). See Tayū (3).

HIMEGIMI 姫君 (lit., miss princess). (1) In Waley, the daughter of Tamakazura; loved by Yūgiri's youngest son, Kurōdo-no-Shōshō; she marries the Retired Emperor Reizei. In Seidensticker, she is just referred to as "the older daughter." (2) In Seidensticker, the name Himegimi is applied to Ukifune's pampered stepsister who marries Sakon.

HITACHI, THE GOVERNOR OF 常陸介 Hitachi-no-suke (lit., the vice-governor of the province of Hitachi). The stepfather of Ukifune who does not care very much for her; he had become something of a country bumpkin.

HOTARU, PRINCE 螢宮 Hotaru-no-miya (lit., prince fireflies). Title of Chapter 25. Seidensticker's name for the half brother of Genji who unsuccessfully courts Tamakazura; he later marries Makibashira. In Waley, he is known as Prince Sochi.

HYŌBU, PRINCE 兵部卿宮 Hyōbukyō-no-miya (lit., prince director of the ministry of military affairs). The brother of Fujitsubo, and the father of Murasaki and the mad wife of Higekuro; a rank later occupied by Niou. In Waley, he is known as Prince Hyōbukyō.

ICHI-NO-MIYA. See First Princess.

IMŌTO 妹尼 Imōto-ama (lit., younger sister/the nun). See Ono, Nun of.

IYO-NO-SUKE 伊豫介 (lit., vice-governor of the province of Iyo). The cuckolded husband of Utsusemi.

JIJŪ 侍從 (lit., chamberlain). (1) The precocious maid who writes Suetsumu Hana's letters. (2) The third son of Tamakazura, known as "the chamberlain" in Seidensticker. (3) The name of a countrified woman in attendance upon Ukifune.

JŌKYŌDEN, LADY 承香殿 Shōkyōden (lit., informed fragrance hall). Named after the imperial hall (see p. 179), a consort of the Suzaku emperor. In Seidensticker, she is called Shōkyōden.

KANNON 観音菩薩 Kannon Bosatsu (in Sanskrit, *Avalokiteshvara*). The Buddhist manifestation of mercy and compassion, usually personified as a woman.

KAORU 薫中將 Kaoru Chūjō (lit., fragrant captain). Supposedly the son of Genji and Nyōsan, the Third Princess of Suzaku; in reality he is the son of Kashiwagi and Nyōsan. Mysteriously, his body is the source of a wonderful fragrance, hence his name. A calm, serious sort, he is the romantic hero of the last ten chapters.

KASHIWAGI 柏木 (lit., the oak tree). Title of Chapter 36. The eldest son of Tō-no-Chūjō, he is a dear friend of Yūgiri. Originally he is married to the Second Princess of Suzaku, Ochiba; he has a clandestine affair with Nyōsan, fathers Kaoru, and dies young.

KINJŌ. See Emperors and Empresses (4).

KII-NO-KAMI 紀伊守 (lit., governor of the province of Kii). (1) An early friend of Genji and participant in the rainy night conversation of Chapter 2, he is the son of Iyo-no-suke and the stepson of Utsusemi. (2) A grandson of the old nun at Ono who is somehow indebted to Kaoru.

KIRITSUBO 桐壺 (lit., paulownia apartments; see p. 179). Title of Chapter 1; the apartments of the old emperor (see Emperors and Empresses, 1) and, therefore, the name given to a frail beauty much loved by him. With no family connections at court, she is only a concubine (see Kōi, below) and as such, is made to suffer the jealousy of the powerful Lady Kokiden and others until she sickens and dies shortly after the birth of her famous son, Genji.

KITA-NO-KATA 北の方 (lit., person of the north). The Heian term for a courtier's principal wife, so called because she would normally occupy the northern wing of his mansion. For example, first Aoi, then Murasaki, and finally Nyōsan, the Third Princess, occupy this position to Genji.

KŌBAI 紅梅 (lit., rose plum). Title of Chapter 43. The younger brother of Kashiwagi; he survives Kashiwagi to become the head of the Fujiwara clan after his father, Tō-no-Chūjō.

KOGIMI 小君 (lit., little one). The young boy who is brother to Utsusemi; he acts as go-between for Genji.

KŌI 更式 (lit., kimono night-watch). A rank assigned to imperial courtesans of lower birth or less powerfully connected family; for example, Kiritsubo.

KOJIJŪ 小侍従 (lit., lesser chamberlain). A maid in the service of Nyōsan, the Third Princess of Suzaku.

KOKIDEN 弘徽殿 (lit., broad, beautiful hall). One of the imperial apartments (see p. 179) and (1) therefore the name applied to the original consort of the old emperor. She is the mother of the heir apparent, Suzaku, and presumes that she will be the empress, but is supplanted first by Kiritsubo, then by Fujitsubo. She is Genji's adversary throughout her life. (2) A name sometimes applied to Tō-no-Chūjō's daughter, Chū-jō, because she later inhabits the imperial apartments of the same name.

KOMOKI こもき (phonetic value only). A young girl left to attend Ukifune at Ono.

KOREMITSU 惟光 (lit., reflected brilliance). Genji's most trusted and faithful retainer.

KOREMITSU'S DAUGHTER 藤典侍 Tō tenji (lit., maid of honor to the Fujiwara). As a maid of honor to the Fujiwara, she is a conquest of Yūgiri's, and in the course of time, mothers six of his twelve or more children.

KOSAISHŌ 小宰相 (lit., lesser councillor). A lady-in-waiting of the First Princess of the Akashi empress; she was once intimate with Kaoru and is again of interest to him after Ukifune's disappearance.

KOZERI. A curious name used by Waley which is not identifiable, as such, in the Japanese text. See Naka-no-kimi (2).

KUMOI, LADY 雲井雁 Kumoi-no-kari (lit., wild goose in the clouds). As the daughter of Tō-no-Chūjō, she is discouraged from accepting the suit of the ardent young Yūgiri, whom she loves. They are eventually wed. Seidensticker calls her Kumoi-no-kari.

KURŌDO-NO-SHŌSHŌ 藏人小將 (lit., guard's lieutenant). (1) Tō-no-Chūjō's brother, who pays court to Nokiba-no-ogi. (2) In Waley, this is the name given to Yūgiri's youngest son by Lady Kumoi; he falls hopelessly in love with Tamakazura's eldest daughter. In Seidensticker, he is called only by his rank, initially lieutenant, then captain.

LOCUST SHELL, LADY OF THE. See Utsusemi.

MAITREYA 彌勒菩薩 Miroku Bosatsu (in Sanskrit, *Maitreya*). The Buddhist manifestation (Bodhisattva) who is to come as a sort of Buddhist messiah in the future.

MAKIBASHIRA 眞木柱 (lit., cypress pillar). Title of Chapter 31. In Waley, this sobriquet is erroneously assigned to Higekuro's demented wife; in Seidensticker, it is correctly given as the daughter of Higekuro and that wife. She is married first to the aging Prince Hotaru and, after his death, to Kōbai.

MICHISADA 道定 (lit., path setter). A privy secretary and son-in-law of Nakanobu, Kaoru's retainer; he is enlisted by Niou to spy on Kaoru.

MIMBU 民部 (from the ministry of popular affairs). A lanky maidservant to Utsusemi.

MINISTER OF THE LEFT 左大臣 Sa-Daijin (lit., great minister of the left). Up to Chapter 19, this rank is held by the father of Lady Aoi and Tō-no-Chūjō and patriarch of the Fujiwara family.

MIYA-NO-KIMI 宮の君 (lit., palace maiden). The beloved daughter of Prince Shikibu (Genji's half brother) who, after her father's death, is forced to go into service. In rank and beauty she is said to resemble Ukifune, and, therefore, she excites the sympathy of Kaoru.

MOKU-NO-KIMI 木工君 (lit., miss woodworker). One of Higekuro's wife's attendants.

MOMOZONO, PRINCE 桃園式部卿 Momozono Shikibukyō (lit., peach-garden prince, director of the ministry of rites). The father of Asagao and the brother of the old emperor; hence Genji's half uncle.

MURASAKI, LADY 紫の上 Murasaki-no-ue (lit., lady
lavender/purple; the color of wisteria). She is the
abandoned daughter of Prince Hyōbu; she is raised and
kept by Genji as his second wife. She may be thought
of as a romantic heroine of the novel; from this
character the author of the Tale is given her name.

MYŌBU 命婦 (lit., royal command woman; of the fifth
rank or above). A lady at court who introduces Genji
to Suetsumu Hana. In Seidensticker, she is known as
Tayū.

NAISHI 内侍 (lit., interior palace attendant). In Seidensticker, this is the name given to the elderly Lady of
the Bedchamber who makes ludicrous passes at young
Genji. She is encountered twice: in Chapter 7 and
in Chapter 20.

NAKANOBU 仲信 (lit., intermediary). One of Kaoru's
trusted retainers whose son-in-law, Michisada, ends
up spying on him for Niou.

NAKA-NO-KIMI 中君 (lit., miss middle). (1) In Waley,
the second daughter of Kōbai in whom he tries unsuccessfully to interest Niou; Seidensticker just calls
her "younger daughter." (2) Seidensticker's name for
the younger of the Prince Hachi's two recognized
daughters; one of the Uji princesses who marries
Niou. Waley calls her Kozeri.

NAKATSUKASA 中務 (lit., from the ministry of central
affairs). (1) A prince and brother to Niou, son of the
Akashi empress and Emperor Kinjō. (2) A common
name for serving women in attendance upon such ladies
as Aoi, Oborozukiyo, and Murasaki.

NIOU, PRINCE 匂の宮 Niou-no-miya (lit., his perfumed highness). Title of Chapter 42. The third son of Emperor Kinjō and the Akashi empress. He has hopes of succeeding his older brother to the throne, but he is a wild rake always involved in scandals. He is a sporting friend and rival to Kaoru in the last ten chapters.

NOKIBA-NO-OGI 軒端の荻 (lit., sedge upon the eaves). Kii-no-kami's sister and the vivacious chess companion to Utsusemi.

NYŌGO, PRINCESS 女五宮 Nyōgo-no-miya (lit., fifth princess). In Waley, Asagao's aunt; she is a younger sister of the old emperor and Princess Ōmiya.

NYŌGO 女御 (lit., woman of the court). A court rank assigned to imperial concubines capable of fathering imperial heirs.

NYŌSAN 女三宮 Onna San-no-miya (lit., third princess). Waley's name for the third and most favored daughter of Emperor Suzaku. She is forced to marry the aging Genji; she has one child, Kaoru, and shortly thereafter becomes a nun. In Seidensticker, she is known as the Third Princess.

OBOROZUKIYO 朧月夜 (lit., night of the misty moon). A sister of Lady Kokiden, she is betrothed to Emperor Suzaku and wooed by Genji, and later becomes Suzaku's empress.

OCHIBA 落葉宮 Ochiba-no-miya (lit., princess fallen leaf). Otherwise known as Onna Ni-no-miya, the second daughter of Emperor Suzaku, she is married off to Kashiwagi. After his death, she is courted by Yūgiri. In Seidensticker, she is called the Second Princess.

ŌIGIMI 大君 (lit., principal daughter). (1) Waley uses this name for Kōbai's eldest daughter, who is given as a consort to the crown prince. (2) See Agemaki.

ŌMI, LADY FROM 近江の君 Ōmi-no-kimi (lit., miss from Ōmi). The obnoxious, long-lost daughter of Tō-no-Chūjō; she was found by accident when he was searching for Yūgao's child, Tamakazura.

ŌMIYA, PRINCESS 大宮 Ōmiya (lit., great princess). The mother of Lady Aoi and Tō-no-Chūjō; she consoles Yūgiri and Kumoi(-no-kari), her two grandchildren.

OMOTO 御許 (lit., of the imperial household). In Waley, a gentlewoman of the elder daughter of Tamakazura; she is sympathetic to Yūgiri's son. In Seidensticker, she is called Chūjō.

ŌMYŌBU 王命婦 (lit., royal command woman; of the fifth rank or above). In Prince Hyōbu's household, she is Fujitsubo's maid who arranges the affair between her lady and Genji.

ONO, NUN OF 小野の尼 Ono-no-ama (lit., the nun of Ono). The younger sister of Sōzu, the Bishop of Yokawa, she is the protector of Ukifune whom she adopts to take the place of her own dead daughter. In Waley, she is called Imōto.

ORANGE BLOSSOMS, LADY OF THE. See Hanachiru Sato.

REIKEIDEN, LADY 麗景殿 Reikeiden (lit., beautiful view hall). Named after the imperial apartments (see p. 179); a consort of Genji's father. See also Hanachiru Sato.

REIZEI. See Emperors and Empresses (3).

ROKUJŌ, LADY 六條の上 Rokujō-no-ue (lit., lady of

the sixth ward). (1) The older woman whom Genji was courting and who subsequently becomes insanely jealous of his other affairs. She was married to a former crown prince (who died) and is, therefore, referred to in the original text as Miyasudokoro 御息所. Akikonomu is her daughter. (2) Rokujō is also the palace Genji builds in his retiring years to house and protect all of his ladies; later taken over by Yūgiri.

ROKU-NO-KIMI 六君 (lit., the sixth daughter). The sixth daughter of Yūgiri by Koremitsu's daughter; she is forced upon Niou.

RYŌZEN. See Emperors and Empresses (3).

SAEMON 左衛門 (lit., left outer-palace guard). A trusted nun left to watch over Ukifune at Ono. In Waley, the name is Sayemon.

SAFFLOWER PRINCESS. See Suetsumu Hana.

SAHYŌE 左兵衛督 Sahyōe-no-kami (lit., left palace guard). A brother of Lady Murasaki who holds a guards commission and is among those who court Tamakazura. In Waley, he is Sahyoye.

SAISHŌ 宰相 (lit., councillor). (1) Yūgiri's nurse. (2) One of Tamakazura's maids.

SAKON 左近 (lit., left palace watch). In Waley, the name of the brash young lieutenant who at first courts Ukifune then rejects her in favor of the Governor of Hitachi's blood-daughter.

SANJŌ 三條 (lit., third ward). (1) The place where Lady Aoi lived and therefore a name used to refer to her. (2) A lady-in-waiting to Yūgao who, after Yūgao's death, accompanies Tamakazura's nurse to Kyūshū.

SECOND PRINCESS 女二宮 Onna Ni-no-miya (lit., the second princess). (1) See Ochiba. (2) The second daughter of Emperor Kinjō by a lesser consort; she is married off to Kaoru.

SHII-NO-SHŌSHŌ 四位少将 (lit., fourth lieutenant). The brother of Lady Kokiden and Lady Oborozukiyo.

SHIKIBU, PRINCE 式部卿宮 Shikibukyō-no-miya (lit., prince director of the ministry of rites). A position held by Genji's half uncle, Prince Momozono, and later by Genji's half brother, the father of Miya-no-kimi.

SHŌKYŌDEN, LADY. See Jōkyōden.

SHŌNAGON 少納言 (lit., minor councillor). The young Murasaki's nurse.

SHŌNI 少弐 (minor assistant of governor general). In Waley, the Deputy Viceroy of Kyūshū who marries Tamakazura's nurse; he affectionately sees to Tamakazura's upbringing and protection.

SHŌSHŌ 少将 (lit., minor commander or lieutenant). (1) A lady-in-waiting to Kozeri. (2) A nun proficient at *koto* in the service of the nun at Ono; previously a lady in attendance to her daughter.

SOCHI, PRINCE 師の宮 Sochi-no-miya (lit., prince governor general). See Hotaru.

SŌZU 横川僧都 Yokawa Sōzu (Sōzu is a Buddhist clerical title somewhat analogous to abbot or bishop). The Bishop of Yokawa on Mt. Hiei, a sainted cleric in his sixties who is renowned as an exorcist. He discovers Ukifune and later ordains her as a nun.

SUETSUMU HANA 末摘花 (lit., tipped safflower or saffron flower). Title of Chapter 6. The quaint lady of noble lineage who is, after all, rather inelegant and has a large, red nose. Genji courts her until he discovers her deformity. In Waley, it is spelled Suyetsumu (Hana); Seidensticker calls her "the safflower princess."

SUMIYOSHI, GOD OF 住吉の神 Sumiyoshi-no-kami (lit., god of abiding fortune). A famous Shintō deity enshrined near Suma and Akashi; the deity responsible, therefore, for the restoration of Genji's fortune after his exile at Suma.

SUZAKU. See Emperors and Empresses (2).

TAMAKAZURA 玉鬘 (lit., the jeweled chaplet). Title of Chapter 22. In Waley, it is rendered as Tamakatsura. The long-lost daughter of Tō-no-Chūjō by Yūgao who is raised in Kyūshū; later found by Genji and presented as if she were his daughter.

TAYŪ 大輔 (lit., senior assistant-minister). (1) In Seidensticker, the lady who helps Genji meet "the safflower princess"; Waley calls her Myōbu. (2) Later, in Seidensticker, a lady in attendance upon Naka-no-kimi. (3) In Waley, it is the name of the gregarious bumpkin from Higo who pursues Tamakazura. (4) Also in Waley, Kōbai's son by Makibashira.

THIRD PRINCESS. See Nyōsan.

TOKIKATA 時方 (lit., time person). Governor of Izumo who, in the Ten Quires of Uji, is a trusted retainer and emissary for Niou.

TŌ-NO-CHŪJŌ 頭の中將 (lit., the first secretary's captain). The brother of Lady Aoi and later the patriarch of the Fujiwara clan; he is throughout the novel a foil to Genji, being his principal friend and rival in all things amorous and artistic.

TŌ SHIKIBU-NO-JŌ 藤式部丞 (lit., Fujiwara func-
tionary from the ministry of rites). One of the young
gallants who joins in the rainy night conversation.

UDONERI 内舎人 (lit., official retainer). A brusque re-
sident of Uji who, as a retainer of Kaoru, is responsible
for guarding Ukifune.

UJI PRINCESSES. See Agemaki; Naka-no-kimi (2) or
Kozeri.

UKIFUNE 浮舟 (lit., boat upon the waters). Title of Chapter 51. The unrecognized daughter of Prince Hachi
and a consort; and, therefore, half sister to the Uji
princesses, Agemaki and Kozeri.

UKON 右近 (lit., right palace watch). (1) The brother of
Kii-no-kami and a faithful retainer of Genji. (2) The
maid of Yūgao taken care of by Genji after Yūgao's
death. (3) A lady-in-waiting to Kozeri. (4) A lady-in-
waiting to Ukifune.

UMA-NO-KAMI. See Hidari Uma-no-kami.

UMETSUBO 梅壺 (lit., plum apartments). See Akikonomu.

UTSUSEMI 空蟬 (lit., locust shell). Title of Chapter 3.
She is the wife of the Vice-Governor of Iyo (Iyo-no-
suke). Genji tries unsuccessfully to repeat her seduc-
tion. Seidensticker calls her "the lady of the locust
shell."

WAKAGIMI 若君 (lit., young miss). In Waley, Tamakazura's younger daughter.

YOKAWA, BISHOP OF. See Sōzu.

YOSHIKIYO 良清 (lit., proper clarity). A former Minamoto councillor (Gen Shōnagon), one of Genji's faithful retainers who goes into exile with him. He had once himself courted the Akashi lady.

YŪGAO 夕顔 (lit., evening face). Title of Chapter 4. The name of a flower applied to the frail beauty and past conquest of Tō-no-Chūjō. Genji woos her, but shortly she dies of demonic possession.

YŪGIRI 夕霧 (lit., evening mist). Title of Chapter 38. Genji's first son by his first wife Lady Aoi. As Genji's principal heir, he fathers more than twelve children and lives a long and prosperous life.

ZEMBŌ, CROWN PRINCE 前坊 Zembō (lit., the earlier one). The name Waley uses for the deceased husband of Lady Rokujō. He has died before the novel opens, but it is clear he was once the heir apparent to the throne and, had he lived, would have been emperor instead of his brother, Emperor Kiritsubo.

2. *Comparative Age Charts*

At the beginning of each of the summaries for Chapters 1–41, there is a note giving the time relative to Genji's age. At the beginning of the remaining Chapters 42–54, the time is given relative to that of Kaoru or Niou. To allow the reader to calculate some of the other main characters' ages, here is a set of three tables relating their ages to first Genji's and then Kaoru's.

Genji	Aoi	Murasaki	Fujitsubo	Rokujō	Akashi lady
17	21	9	22	24	8

Genji	Yūgiri	Tamakazura	Kashiwagi	Nyōsan (Third Princess)
40	19	26	24	14

Kaoru	Niou	Ukifune	Kozeri (Naka-no-kimi)	Agemaki (Ōigimi)	Akashi princess (later empress)
24	25	19	24	26	43

Note that there can be no overlapping of ages, as the Japanese did not record or celebrate the day or month of birth. People are one year old at birth, and everyone becomes a year older on New Year's Day. As a result, individual birthdays are not celebrated annually. Instead, specific longevity landmarks in one's life are honored, such as the celebrations in Chapter 34, "Wakana: Jo," when Genji attains his fortieth year.

3. *Maps of Places Mentioned*

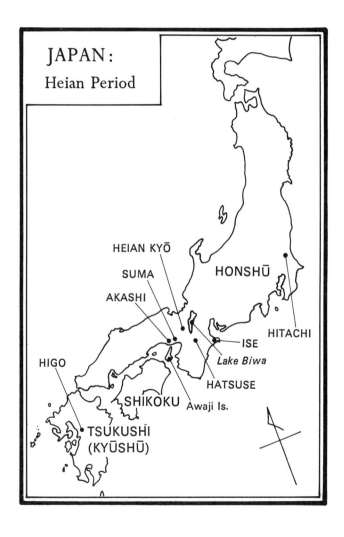

JAPAN:
Heian Period

HEIAN KYŌ
SUMA
AKASHI
HONSHŪ
HITACHI
ISE
Lake Biwa
HIGO
HATSUSE
SHIKOKU Awaji Is.
TSUKUSHI
(KYŪSHŪ)

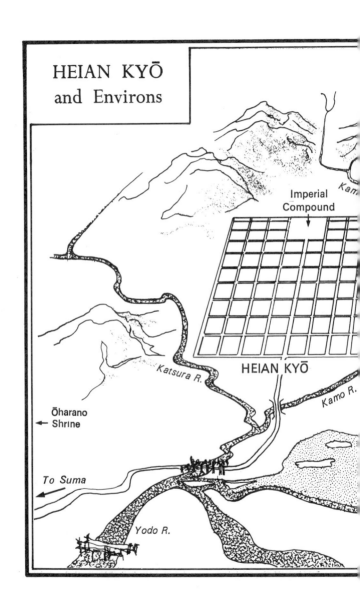

HEIAN KYŌ
and Environs

Imperial
Compound

Kam

HEIAN KYŌ

Katsura R.

Kamo R.

Ōharano
← Shrine

To Suma
←

Yodo R.

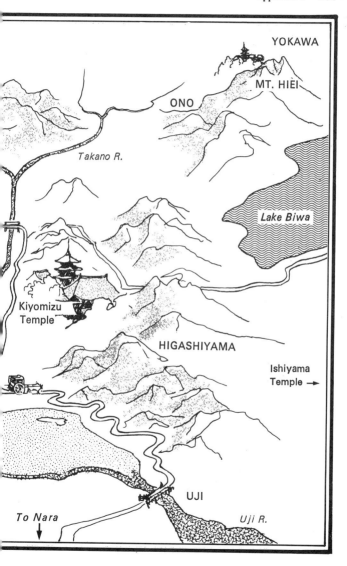

YOKAWA

MT. HIĒI

ONO

Takano R.

Lake Biwa

Kiyomizu
Temple

HIGASHIYAMA

Ishiyama
Temple →

To Nara

UJI

Uji R.

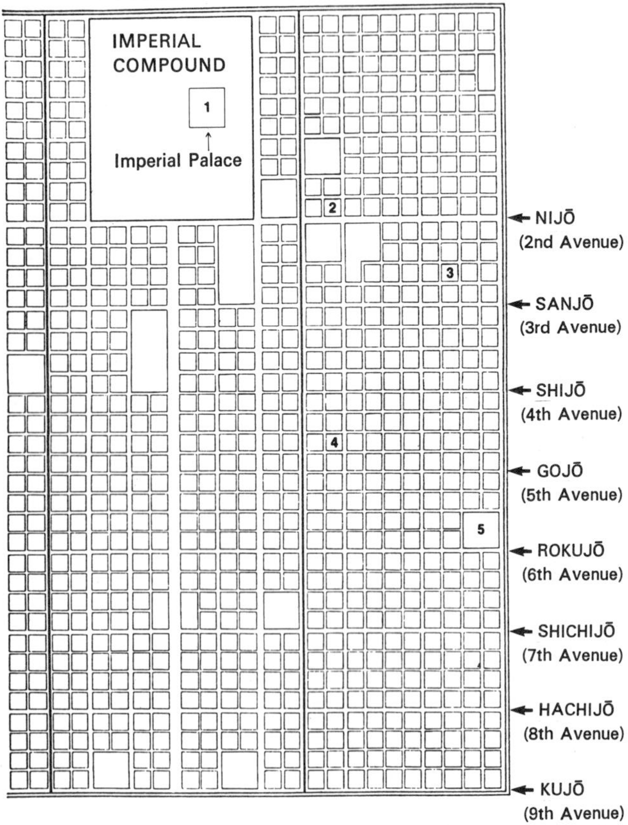

IMPERIAL
COMPOUND

1

↑
Imperial Palace

◄— NIJŌ
(2nd Avenue)

◄— SANJŌ
(3rd Avenue)

◄— SHIJŌ
(4th Avenue)

◄— GOJŌ
(5th Avenue)

◄— ROKUJŌ
(6th Avenue)

◄— SHICHIJŌ
(7th Avenue)

◄— HACHIJŌ
(8th Avenue)

◄— KUJŌ
(9th Avenue)

Street map of the left side and center of Heian Kyō. Since the Tale is based on life in the Heian capital, it is possible to calculate the approximate location of places mentioned in the novel. 1. Imperial palace (detailed on facing page); 2. Genji's Nijō palace, where he lives in the early chapters; 3. Aoi's Sanjō mansion, later occupied by Yūgiri and Kumoi; 4. Yūgao's home; 5. Lady Rokujō's estate, later enlarged and developed into Genji's Rokujō mansion.

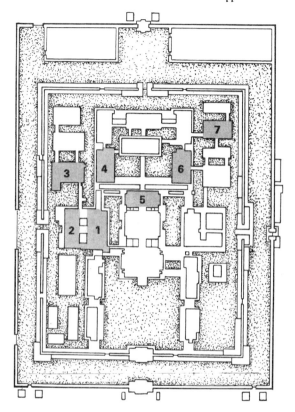

Plan of the actual imperial palace buildings. The movements of the courtiers described in the Tale were made to coincide with the actual design of the buildings at that time. Note the long, unavoidable walk past the Kokiden (4), that Lady Kiritsubo had to make from her apartment (7) on her way to Seiryōden (1), the emperor's private quarters (as described in the first chapter). Later, she was moved to Kōrōden (2), in order to be closer to the emperor. Fujitsubo's residence is (3), Shōkyōden (5), Reikeiden (6).

Notes

INTRODUCTION

1. Edwin Cranston, "The Seidensticker Genji." *Journal of Japanese Studies*, 4 (1978) 1: 1–25.

SECTION I

1. Ivan Morris, *The World of the Shining Prince* (New York: Alfred A. Knopf, 1964), p. 153.

2. John Whitney Hall, *Japan from Prehistory to Modern Times* (New York: Dell Publishing, 1971), p. 50.

3. Murasaki Shikibu, *The Tale of Genji,* tr. Edward G. Seidensticker, 2 vols. (New York: Alfred A. Knopf, 1976), 2, p. 558.

4. *Ibid.,* p. 553.

5. *Ibid.,* p. 600.

SECTION II

1. For an excellent summary and a commentary on this sutra, see the essay "The Lotus Sutra" by Wing-Tsit Chang, in *Approaches to the Oriental Classics,* ed. Wm. Theodore de Bary (New York: Columbia University Press, 1959).

SECTION III

1. Morris, *The World of the Shining Prince,* pp. 318–19.

2. Arthur Waley, *Japanese Poetry: The Uta* (1919; reprinted ed., Honolulu: University Press of Hawaii, 1976), p. 105.

3. *The Tale of Genji*, tr. Seidensticker, l, p. 254n.

4. R. Tsunoda, D. Keene, Wm. T. de Bary, *Introduction to Oriental Civilization*, vol. 1, *Sources of Japanese Tradition* (New York: Columbia University Press, 1958), p. 172.

5. Earl Miner, *An Introduction to Japanese Court Poetry* (Stanford: Stanford University Press), p. 161.

6. Miner, "Some Thematic and Structural Features of the Genji Monogatari." *Monumenta Nipponica*, XXIV (1969) 1: 1.

7. Murasaki Shikibu, *The Izumi Shikibu Diary*, tr. Edwin Cranston, Harvard Yenching Institute's Monograph Series, 19 (Cambridge, Mass.: Harvard University Press, 1969), pp. 232–33.

8. Sen'ichi Hisamatsu, *The Vocabulary of Japanese Literary Aesthetics* (Tokyo: The Centre of East Asian Cultural Studies, 1963), p. 103.

9. Masaharu Anesaki, *Art, Life and Nature in Japan* (1932; reprinted ed., Rutland and Tokyo: Tuttle, 1973), p. 65.

10. Amy Lowell, "Introduction" to *Diaries of Court Ladies in Old Japan*, trs. Annie S. Omori and Kochi Doi (Boston: Houghton Mifflin Co., 1920), pp. xxii–xxiii.

11. Murasaki Shikibu, *The Tale of Genji*, tr. Arthur Waley (1935; reprinted ed., New York: Random House, 1960), p. 264.

12. *The Tale of Genji*, tr. Seidensticker, 1, p. 254.

13. *Ibid.*

SECTION IV

1. *Diaries of Court Ladies*, trs. Omori and Doi, p. 105–6.

2. *Ibid.*, p. 94.

3. *Ibid.*, p. 134.

SECTION V

1. Morris, "The Genius of Arthur Waley" in *Madly Singing*

in the Mountains, ed. Morris (New York: Walker and Co., 1970), p. 71.

2. Keene, "In Your Distant Street Few Drums Were Heard" in *Madly Singing in the Mountains,* p. 58.

3. Cranston, *Journal of Japanese Studies,* 4 (1978) 1: 1–25.

SECTION VI

1. *The Tale of Genji,* tr. Waley, p. 139n.

2. Seidensticker, *Genji Days* (New York: Harper and Row, 1977), p. 86.

3. *The Tale of Genji,* tr. Seidensticker, 2, p. 641n.

4. *Op. cit.,* tr. Seidensticker, 2, p. 530; tr. Waley, p. 606.

5. *Op. cit.,* tr. Seidensticker, 2, p. 608; tr. Waley, pp. 651–52.

6. *Op. cit.,* tr. Waley, p. 174.

7. *Op. cit.,* tr. Seidensticker, 1, p. 176.

SECTION VII

1. *The Tale of Genji,* tr. Waley, Part 4, Ch. 3.

SECTION VIII

1. Murasaki Shikibu, *The Bridge of Dreams,* tr. Waley (Boston: Houghton Mifflin Co., 1933), Introduction.

2. *Ibid.,* p. 33.

3. Seidensticker, *Genji Days,* p. 51.

Bibliography

ENGLISH TRANSLATIONS
of *Genji Monogatari* by Murasaki Shikibu
(in chronological order with the length of each work given)

Genji Monogatari. Trans. in part Kenchō Suematsu. London: Colonial Press, 1900; reprinted ed., Rutland and Tokyo: Charles E. Tuttle Company, 1975. (227 pp.)

The Tale of Genji, Part I. Trans. Arthur Waley. Boston: Houghton Mifflin Company, 1925 (300 pp.); reprinted ed., Garden City, New York: Doubleday and Company, 1955. (253 pp.)

The Sacred Tree, Part II. Trans. Arthur Waley. Boston: Houghton Mifflin Company, 1926. (304 pp.)

A Wreath of Cloud, Part III. Trans. Arthur Waley. Boston: Houghton Mifflin Company, 1927. (312 pp.)

Blue Trousers, Part IV. Trans. Arthur Waley. Boston: Houghton Mifflin Company, 1928. (339 pp.)

The Lady of the Boat, Part V. Trans. Arthur Waley. Boston: Houghton Mifflin Company, 1932. (309 pp.)

The Bridge of Dreams: Being the Second Part of "The Lady of the Boat" and the Final Part of "The Tale of Genji." Trans. Arthur Waley. Boston: Houghton Mifflin Company, 1933. (341 pp.)

The Tale of Genji: A Novel in Six Parts. Trans. Arthur Waley. Boston: Houghton Mifflin Company, 1935. Reprinted eds., New York: Random House, 1960; London: George Allen and

Unwin Limited, 1967; Tokyo: Charles E. Tuttle Company, 1970. (1135 pp.)

The Tale of Genji. Trans. Edward G. Seidensticker, 2 vols. (hard-cover) or 1 vol. (softcover). New York: Alfred A. Knopf, 1976; Tokyo: Charles E. Tuttle Company, 1978. (1090 pp.)

BOOKS ABOUT "THE TALE OF GENJI" AND HEIAN PERIOD

Anesaki, Masaharu. *Art, Life and Nature in Japan.* Boston: Marshall Jones Company, 1932; reprinted ed., Rutland and Tokyo: Charles E. Tuttle Company, 1973.

Aston, W. G. *A History of Japanese Literature.* New York: Heinemann, 1899; reprinted ed., Rutland and Tokyo: Charles E. Tuttle Company, 1972.

Brower, Robert H. and Miner, Earl. *Japanese Court Poetry.* Stanford, California: Stanford University Press, 1961.

Chamberlain, Basil Hall. *Japanese Things.* London: Kegan Paul, 1905; reprinted ed., Rutland and Tokyo: Charles E. Tuttle Company, 1971.

de Bary, Wm. Theodore, ed. *The Buddhist Tradition in India, China, and Japan.* New York: Random House, 1969.

Harich-Schneider, Eta. *A History of Japanese Music.* London: Oxford University Press, 1973.

Hisamatsu, Sen'ichi, et al. *Murasaki Shikibu: The Greatest Lady Writer in Japanese Literature.* Tokyo: The Japanese National Commission for UNESCO, 1970.

_____. *The Vocabulary of Japanese Literary Aesthetics.* Tokyo: Centre for East Asian Cultural Studies, 1963.

Janeira, Armando Martins. *Japanese and Western Literature: A Comparative Study.* Rutland and Tokyo: Charles E. Tuttle Company, 1970.

Kokusai Bunka Shinkokai (The Society for International Cultural Relations). *Introduction to Classical Japanese Literature.* Tokyo: K.B.S., 1948.

Malm, William P. *Japanese Music and Musical Instruments.* Rutland and Tokyo: Charles E. Tuttle Company, 1959.

Miner, Earl. *An Introduction to Japanese Court Poetry*. Stanford, California: Stanford University Press, 1968.

Morris, Ivan. *The World of The Shining Prince: Court Life in Ancient Japan*. Baltimore, Maryland: Penguin Books, 1964.

_____, trans. and ed. *The Pillow Book of Sei Shonagon*. Baltimore, Maryland: Penguin Books, 1967.

_____, trans. *The Tale of Genji, Scroll*. Tokyo: Kodansha International, 1971.

_____, ed. *Madly Singing in the Mountains: An Appreciation of Arthur Waley*. New York: Walker and Company, 1970.

Omori, Annie Shepley and Doi, Kochi, trans. *Diaries of Court Ladies of Old Japan*. Boston: Houghton Mifflin Company, 1920.

Reischauer, Jean and Robert Karl. *Early Japanese History*. Princeton, New Jersey: Princeton University Press, 1937.

Rimer, Thomas J. *Modern Japanese Fiction and Its Traditions: An Introduction*. Princeton, New Jersey: Princeton University Press, 1978.

Seidensticker, Edward G. *Genji Days*. Tokyo: Kodansha International; New York: Harper and Row, 1977.

_____. *This Country, Japan*. Tokyo: Kodansha International; New York: Harper and Row, 1979.

Ueda, Makoto. *Literary and Art Theories in Japan*. Cleveland, Ohio: The Press of Western Reserve University, 1967.

ARTICLES ABOUT "THE TALE OF GENJI"

Abe, Akio. "Murasaki Shikibu's View on the Nature of Monogatari." *Acta Asiatica* 11 (1966): 1–10.

Cranston, Edwin. "Murasaki's 'Art of Fiction.' " *Japan Quarterly* XVIII (1971) 2: 207–13.

_____. "The Seidensticker Genji." *Journal of Japanese Studies* 4 (1978) 1: 1–25.

Gatten, Aileen. "A Wisp of Smoke: Scent and Character in *The Tale of Genji*." *Monumenta Nipponica* XXXII (1977) 1: 35–48.

Keene, Donald. "The Tale of Genji" in *Approaches to the Oriental*

Classics, Wm. Theodore de Bary, ed., 186–95. New York and London: Columbia University Press, 1959.

Maki, J. M. "Lady Murasaki and The Genji Monogatari." *Monumenta Nipponica* III (1940) 2: 120–43.

Mano, Ayako. "Tale of Genji." *The East* I (1964) 2: 30–35.

McCullough, Helen. "The Seidensticker Genji." *Monumenta Nipponica* XXXII (1977) 1: 93–110.

McCullough, William. "Japanese Marriage Institutions in the Heian Period." *Harvard Journal of Asiatic Studies* 27 (1967): 103–67.

Miner, Earl. "Some Thematic and Structural Features of the Genji Monogatari." *Monumenta Nipponica* XXIV (1969) 1–2: 1–19.

_____. "The Rise of the Radiant Prince." *Times Literary Supplement,* 28 Jan. 1977: 98.

Miyoshi, Masao. "Translation as Interpretation." *Journal of Asian Studies* XXXVIII (1979) 2: 299–302.

Mudrick, Marvin. "Genji and the Age of Marvels." *Hudson Review* VIII (1955) 3: 327–45.

Nichols, James R. "The Tale of Genji: A Novel of Manners, A.D. 1020." *Japan Quarterly* XVI (1970) 2: 178–81.

Oyama, Atsuko. "How Was the Genji Monogatari Written?" *Acta Asiatica* 2 (1961): 59–68.

Seidensticker, Edward G. "A Decade or So for the *Genji.*" *Delos* 2 (1968): 126–131.

_____. "Chiefly on Translating the *Genji.*" *Journal of Japanese Studies* 6 (1980) 1: 15–47.

Stinchecum, Amanda Mayer. "Who Tells the Tale? 'Ukifune': A Study in Narrative Voice." *Monumenta Nipponica* XXXV (1980) 4: 375–403.

Takeda, Katsuhiko. "The Tale of Genji: A Review of the Seidensticker Translation." *Japan Quarterly* XXIV (1977) 2: 238–41.

Ury, Marian. "The Imaginary Kingdom and the Translator's Art: Notes on Reading Waley's Genji." *Journal of Japanese Studies* II (1976) 2: 267–94.

_____. "The Complete Genji." *Harvard Journal of Asiatic Studies* 37 (1977) 1: 183–201.

Yashiro, Yukio. "Arthur Waley." *Japan Quarterly* XIV (1967) 3: 365–69.

WORKS IN JAPANESE CONSULTED

Asō, Isoji. *Koten Zukan* (Illustrated Atlas to the Classics). Tōkyō: Meiji Shoin Publishers, 1969.

"Genji Monogatari Emaki Gojūyon-jō." (The 54 Picture Scrolls of *The Tale of Genji*). *Taiyō* (The Sun), Special Issue. ed. Baba Ichirō. No. 3, Summer, 1973.

Ikeda, Kikan, *Genji Monogatari Jiten,* 2 vols. Tōkyō: Tōkyōdō Publishers, 1960.

Ikeda, Yasaburō. *Hikaru Genji no Issei* (Generation of the Shining Genji). Tōkyō: Kōdansha Publishers, 1964.

Murasaki Shikibu. *Genji Monogatari.* Annotated by Yamagishi Tokuhei, 6 vols., Iwanami Bunko Library. Tōkyō: Iwanami Shoten, 1965.

Glossary-Index